Blessings TOO GOOD

Blessings!
Sandi Rauwolf
Aug. '08

BASED ON A TRUE STORY
of GOD'S BLESSINGS TOUCHING A YOUNG FAMILY

SANDI RAUWOLF

xulon
PRESS

Blessings Too Good
by Sandi Rauwolf

Printed in the United States of America

ISBN 978-1-60647-109-8

Library of Congress Cataloging-in-Publication Data

Rauwolf, Sandi, 2007
Blessings Too Good. Based on a true story of God's blessings touching a young family.
Website: www.blessingstoogood.com

Author Photo by: Glamour Shots, Orland Park, IL
Cover/Interior Designed by: Susan Doctor

www.xulonpress.com

Table of Contents

Acknowledgments

This book has been a work in progress for quite a few years. After the first blessing God sent our way, people encouraged me to write a book to share what God had done in my family. Thus the seed was planted. God continued to do unbelievable things in our lives time and time again. With each miracle, at least one person would mention to me that I should write a book, especially since some people don't see even one miracle in their lifetime let alone multiple miracles. It seemed every time the idea of the book was furthest from my mind, God would send us another blessing as a reminder of what could happen when we put our trust in Him. Our son Tyler has been a big inspiration to me. Years before I began writing the book, Ty presented me with the title and made me promise I would use it for my book. That moment was when I committed to writing the book because I knew I couldn't promise my little boy that I would use his title unless I actually wrote the book!

I started the book a few different times, even rewriting it a couple of times, but it seemed life kept getting busy and so I would set it aside. During my most recent surgery in November 2007, my son and I read the great book *90 Minutes in Heaven* by Don Piper. Ty said, "Mom, you need to tell your story so you can touch lives too. You need to finish your book." Thank you, Don, for sharing your story with the world and thus giving me the confidence I needed to share my story. I have always believed that blessings serve as a testimony to God by proving all things are possible with Him. Ty was right; it was time to share my story. So while I was recovering from my recent surgery, I got out my laptop to finish my book.

There are so many people I want to thank, but first I want to say thank you to my husband; without him by my side and the unconditional love he has always shown me I would not have been able to face all that we have endured … thank you to my children, who have served as a daily reminder that every minute of life is a gift because they brighten mine so much … thank you to my father, who listened to the tug on his heart when God asked him to walk away from his career and to so unselfishly be there for us to offer his help, love, support, and anything we needed … thank you to Carrie, who has always puts other people's needs before her own. She has been our earth angel through it all … thank you to my step dad, because without his help and love we would have never been able to call Samantha our daughter … thank you to my mom, who has served as an example of how we are to show compassion and love to others despite some of the hardest challenges we may face in life … thank you to my brother, who encouraged me and supported me with his love and laughter throughout the years; I also want to thank him for sharing his personal story in this book … thank you to my sister, who was by my side every step of the way designing book covers, supporting me spiritually, and always having an open heart and mind to what God was telling her … thank you to Carol Doctor, who was open to the heart tugs God used to bring me support and prayers to get this book published by flooding the Internet with prayer requests for this publication ... thank you to Sandie, who has been like a mom to me and who has always been there to laugh, cry, and rejoice with me through it all ... thank you to Ken Edwards, who has been my spiritual mentor for years. I'm very thankful he allowed God to work through him to help me get back on my spiritual path ... thank you to the rest of our family and friends who have been there when we needed them most ... thank you to the doctors at the University of Chicago, especially Dr. Nadera Sweiss and my hematologist, who kept pressing forward to find treatments for me and instilled hope no matter how challenging my disease became ... thank you to the best church our family has ever found, Parkview Christian Church located in Orland Park, IL, whose pastors and members have unknowingly served as an inspiration through their example of love, compassion, and support to the church members and to the community. Parkview made us feel welcome and like we had finally come home when we first walked through the doors of the church ... thank you to my book editor Janet Angelo, whose assistance was invaluable.

Thank you to God for instilling faith, love, compassion, and peace in my heart, all of which are gifts I feel destined to share with others to help them find the same indescribable peace through Christ. And lastly, I thank God every day for the journey I have traveled so far. Without Him, writing this book would not have been possible.

Life is full of challenges that are critical to our spiritual path. When facing these challenges we have choices that only we can make. We can choose to let life's difficulties break us down and fill us with anger, or we can choose to rise above them and stay true to the person God wants us to be. We can easily give up and run in another direction but by doing that, we will only end up feeling empty and discouraged inside. We need to be thankful for the challenges we face because they are necessary to our spiritual growth, and it's those challenges that bring us closer to the life that God promises each of us.

> *"My dear brothers, take note of this: Everyone should be quick to listen, slow to speak and slow to become angry, for man's anger does not bring about the righteous life that God desires. Therefore, get rid of all moral filth and the evil that is so prevalent and humbly accept the word planted in you, which can save you" (James 1:19-21).*

When we're at a crossroad in life, we will feel a tug on our hearts helping us to make the right choices. When we don't listen to that tug, we stumble and fall. However, we should not dwell on those mistakes because they teach us so much. Until we learn to listen to the tugs of our hearts, we will most likely make some very bad decisions. An important part of being a Christian is recognizing just how imperfect we are and understanding that in Christ, who died for our sins, we are promised eternal life. His death washes away all of our sins, forever bringing us closer to God.

Do not allow difficulties in life to overwhelm you and change the person God intends for you to be. God definitely wants each one of us to have peace and to enjoy an abundant life; therefore, instead of letting life rob you of the peace God wants for you, turn to God during those times. Open your heart to what He is doing in your life, be thankful for the challenges, and trust Him even when the pain is so deep you cannot comprehend why you must endure it.

> *"Do not be anxious about anything, but in everything, by prayer and petition, with thanksgiving, present your requests to God. And the peace of God, which transcends all understanding, will guard your hearts and your minds in Christ Jesus" (Philippians 4:6-7).*

Never lose sight of His promise to all who love Him, and remember: none will be forsaken.

> *"The Lord is a refuge for the oppressed, a stronghold in times of trouble. Those who know your name will trust in you, for you, Lord, have never forsaken those who seek you" (Psalm 9:9-10).*

I was reminded of this one afternoon while my then ten-year-old son Ty and I were driving home. There was a beautiful sunset, and Ty pointed to the sky and said, "Mom, look, there is a cross in the sky!" I looked up and saw that the clouds had formed the shape of a cross against the gorgeous crimson sky. It was magnificent! We started talking about how God could do anything if we were open to the signs around us, just like how He was letting us know He loved us at that very moment by painting the sky with a cross for us to see. We were blessed to have God in our hearts. Suddenly Ty looked at me and said, "Mom, I know what you should call your book."

I looked at him and said, "Book?"

I had not talked about writing my book for some time, although I knew that one day I wanted to share all of the blessings God had done for my family and me. Ty had caught me off guard just now when out of nowhere he'd brought it up again.

He said, "Yes, the book about all of our blessings. You should call it Blessings Too Good."

I said, "What do you mean by Blessings Too Good?"

He said, "Well when you help other people you are bringing blessings to them but then God blesses you back. And what's neat, Mom, is that it seems too good to be true – like all of the miracles that have happened for you!"

I paused for a minute thinking about what he had just said. Here was my excited ten-year-old boy asking, "Do you like it? Do you like it?"

Tears came to my eyes as I mused, what a profound thought for a ten-year-old. Choking back those tears I said, "I love it. It is perfect, just perfect!" At that moment I felt a tug on my heart to start writing this book you are now reading. I had talked about writing it for years … and now it was time. I wanted to share with everyone the blessings only God could have given us. I wanted to encourage you, dear reader, to know that these blessings are possible for you, too – for everyone – even when things seem impossible. By opening up your minds and hearts to God, you will see that there is nothing God cannot do.

"... With man this is impossible, but with God all things are possible." (Matthew 19:26)

In helping you to open your mind and heart to Christ, whether it is the first time or strengthening the bond you already have with Him, I want to share the multiple blessings God has performed in my life. Each serves as a testimony to the unfailing love and promise He has made to everyone who welcomes Christ into his or her heart. The Bible serves as a written testimony to God's work and is incredibly powerful. Some have a difficult time associating those events from Bible times long ago with today's modern world, and many people ask for some sort of proof before they can "believe." But how many of us have blessings all around us that we see and ignore or experience but do not share? Those blessings are the proof that God is alive and real. My story is about such blessings. Some were disguised as hardships and even tests of faith, but no doubt ... all were blessings. Each one of us needs to share the blessings God has given us, both big and small, so that the world will know that God is as real today as He was in Bible times.

CHAPTER 1

Crosses We Must Bear

(Age 21)

"For this reason, since the day we heard about you, we have not stopped praying for you and asking God to fill you with the knowledge of his will through all spiritual wisdom and understanding. ... For he has rescued us from the dominion of darkness and brought us into the kingdom of the Son he loves, in whom we have redemption, the forgiveness of sins" *(Colossians 1:9, 13-14).*

Since childhood, I have done my best to look for the good in every situation no matter how bad things appeared to everyone around me. I did not know at the time what a gift that was and how much I would have to rely on my strong faith to get me through some tough times ahead.

When I was growing up, our family did not attend church every Sunday, but our parents raised us to be polite, clean, and to always say our prayers at night. So, from an early age, I turned to God. Without having a formal religious upbringing,

I did not realize that a mom and dad teaching a little two-year-old girl to fold her hands and pray "Now I lay me down to sleep …" was forming a foundation, and a very important one at that. By teaching me to pray every night my parents were helping me to build a foundation for a lifetime of turning to God and giving Him my troubles.

I am the oldest of three children and was baptized as a baby in the Catholic Church. Our parents struggled with finding a church that they could call home. Their hearts seemed committed to God, but since they could not find a home church we slowly fell into the category of families who went to church mainly around the holidays. My brother and sister were never baptized, and this always bothered me, even at a young age. So we grew up knowing about God, but we didn't quite understand how we could be close to Him, and we didn't realize the peace, love, and happiness we would find once we accepted Him completely into our hearts. None of us, including our parents, would learn that lesson for many more years. Many of those lessons would be learned through my journey.

I'm thankful our parents ensured God was part of our lives. We were constantly reminded of the people we were supposed to be, and we were taught to love others, be compassionate, tell the truth, and to respect people, particularly our elders. When my brother was still a baby my sister and I would board a powder blue school bus every Sunday morning during the summer to attend Bible school. We would patiently (well, most of the time) wait for the bus to arrive. We stood there smiling and standing proudly while we twisted from side-to-side, now and then, so that our dresses would flare out as if they were floating in the air. We felt so pretty in our Sunday best clothes and looked forward to Bible school every week.

My sister and I are one year apart and looked very much alike at the time. (We are actually the same age for four days of every year.) My mom usually dressed us in the same outfits, so everyone thought we were twins. We would sing songs on the way to Bible school to pass the time during the thirty-minute bus ride more quickly. My favorite song was "Jesus Loves Me." You know how it goes. I'm sorry, I know this song will be in your head all day now but, who knows, maybe it is just what you need today!

Jesus Loves Me

Traditional
Words By: Anna B. Warner
Music By: William B. Bradbury
Copyright Unknown

Jesus loves me! This I know,
For the Bible tells me so;
Little ones to Him belong,
They are weak but He is strong.
Yes, Jesus loves me!
Yes, Jesus loves me!
Yes, Jesus loves me!
The Bible tells me so.

Jesus loves me! He who died,
Heaven's gate to open wide;
He will wash away my sin,
Let His little child come in.

Yes, Jesus loves me!
Yes, Jesus loves me!
Yes, Jesus loves me!
The Bible tells me so.

Jesus loves me! loves me still,
When I'm very weak and ill;
From His shining throne on high,
Comes to watch me where I lie.
Yes, Jesus loves me!
Yes, Jesus loves me!
Yes, Jesus loves me!
The Bible tells me so.

Jesus loves me! He will stay,
Close beside me all the way;
He's prepared a home for me,
And some day His face I'll see.
Yes, Jesus loves me!
Yes, Jesus loves me!
Yes, Jesus loves me!
The Bible tells me so.[1]

I didn't realize until I was older just exactly what the words in that song would mean to me. Those simple yet powerful words hold the secret of the life you and I desire to have, the abundant life filled with peace and happiness that God wants for each of us. I knew about God and Jesus, but I did not fully understand who they were at the time.

Even though I grew up in a small Midwest town in Indiana without a lot of luxuries, I believed I was meant to live a life full of happiness and contentment. After attending college, I naively headed toward a Chicago suburb to find a job. Although

I had a short resume and limited experience, I was offered a job based on my drive and determination. I was thrilled! It felt like I was taking the first step toward fulfilling God's plan for my life.

The people I worked with in this first job helped groom me into the person I am today. I am still in close contact with many of them and consider them to be true friends. A few people I met there became very special to me, because they helped me on my spiritual journey. The first to help along that path was Sandie, who has always been like a mom to me. When my parents divorced, my mom moved out of state shortly thereafter. My mother and I remained very close, but she wished she could be here with me, especially when I faced challenges in my life. When Sandie came into my life, she was a blessing not only to me but also to my mom. My mom was thankful that someone was nearby to help me during the times she could not be there, and she believed God sent Sandie along to be this person for me. This would especially become true a few years later when I would face some of the most difficult challenges of my life.

The second person God sent into my life was my co-worker Ken. Everybody loves Ken because he has an enthusiasm and love for life that is absolutely contagious. There is something about him that makes people ask, "What is it about him that makes him so different? What gives him such happiness?" I wanted to have that enthusiasm too. It wasn't until later that I figured out his secret to happiness.

When I first met Ken it was as if I already knew him, as if we were members of the same family. Ken always seemed so "together" and offered good advice to a sometimes pathetic, struggling, young lady – more times than I can remember. We had a lot of laughs, especially when Ken, Sandie, and I would get together for our weekly lunch at the local Chinese restaurant buffet.

I felt like I had known Sandie and Ken my whole life, and I knew I could trust them. Both seemed to sense when I was struggling and knew exactly what to say to help me, Sandie with her motherly support and advice, and Ken with his spiritual guidance. Ken and I had several conversations about faith and praying, but at the time I was struggling in what seemed like every part of my life. I was focusing more on my struggles than my faith and had my ears closed to anything Ken was trying to say to get through to me.

I should have felt like I was on top of the world. I had just moved out of my dad's house and was living with Kim, whom I had also met through work and who became one of my closest friends. I was driving a nice car. I had a great job with wonderful co-workers, but my life still felt empty. I was lonely, not to mention living from paycheck to paycheck. I struggled with finding the good in the situation. Ken was giving me pep talks quite a bit. No matter what he ever faced, his optimism was incredibly positive. But, despite his pep talks, I just wasn't able to relate to his positive enthusiasm and joy for living.

Every day seemed to suck me into more negativity. One day the smallest things collectively ended up being the straw that broke the camel's back. It seemed like anything that could go wrong did! As soon as I got home from work, I put on my pajamas and went to bed, where I cried myself to sleep. I probably asked God fifty times, "How can I be so miserable when I have so many things to be thankful for? Why do I feel so empty? Why is my life going so wrong?!" So there I was asking for God's help, but not fully trusting in Him. I thought I had to fix most of it on my own. Besides, I thought, God is only there to listen to me and not really do anything … right? I did not have any proof that He was going to help me, and so I didn't really believe He would. I eventually drifted off to sleep.

That night I dreamed that God was telling me I needed to focus on my faith, and that until I did I would continue to feel empty despite the blessings in my life. God then brought Ken into my dream, making it very clear to me that he was going to be helping me on my spiritual path and that I was to open my mind and heart to all of it. I realized at that time Ken had been trying to help me but my ears had been closed to him. Despite hearing his words, I had not comprehended them. The dream made me realize I needed to start listening. This revelation was actually comforting, since I knew that Ken, of anyone, would help me find my way. This was, by far, one of the most powerful dreams I had ever had. I woke up and could not go back to sleep. I lay there wondering in the darkness, was it really a dream? Was that the answer? I can't wait to see Ken and tell him!

Upon arriving at work, I hurried down the hall and barged into Ken's office. I was so excited to share with him the powerful dream I had. "You are NEVER going to believe this dream I had last night! God was in it and so were you!" I looked up and saw that he was smiling and nodding knowingly. I explained that just the night before I felt like I was at my end, at one of my weakest moments, and so I began crying out to God trying to understand why I felt so empty inside. "I know it's pathetic," I said, smiling, "but I really did have a bad night. Anyway, after I cried myself to sleep, it was unbelievable, Ken. I get chills just getting ready to tell you this. God was talking to me saying it was important for me to find my faith again. Then, next thing I knew, you were in my dream talking to me about it and helping me with whatever I needed to get back on my spiritual path. Can you believe that?"

He looked at me smiling and said, "I know."

I looked at him and said, "What?"

He said, "That wasn't a dream, Sandi. I felt God telling me the same thing last night. He wants me to help you find your way back to Him. Isn't He wonderful?"

I had chills. I looked at Ken with an expression of amazement and disbelief as thoughts of disbelief whirled through my mind. How in the world did he know? That is not possible! Would someone please pinch me, because I'm obviously still sleeping!? However, I wasn't sleeping. I was fully awake and sitting right there in Ken's office. There was no question that God wanted my attention and believe me, He got it!

Ken had always talked about God with such energy, love, and joy radiating from his soul, and I really wanted to have those same feelings. I wanted that happiness, that peace, but I wondered – was I special enough for God to bless me with them as He had done for my spiritual friend?

I knew Ken had prayed for me a lot. I believe that from the time he met me he felt my struggles, especially the ones relating to my faith as I was trying to follow my spiritual path. He was not surprised God used a dream to make it happen, but I was still in awe at the length God went to in order to get my complete attention. Ken understood the unbelievable things that are possible with God. "There is nothing He cannot do," Ken assured me, and I wanted to believe that but I wasn't quite there yet. I nodded as I listened to him, but in my thoughts I was wondering, are all things really possible – even the impossible things? How can that be? Despite my doubts, however, I had complete trust in Ken's wisdom and his love for God, so I trusted what he shared with me.

That moment was a turning point in my life, a very important one. I had no idea that God would work through other people to help me get back on track when I was at a critical crossroad in my life. I thought there would have to be some miracle of God standing right in front of me to make it all real. But I was beginning to realize that God doesn't present Himself in a physical sense. His spirit is in those all around us working to help us along our way, and this was truly amazing to me!

I walked out of Ken's office feeling a wonderful sense of peace inside. I felt like I could face anything as long as God was with me and I kept my mind and heart open to the people and things God would send my way to help me. I promised myself that I would pray more often and do my best to give my troubles and my worries to God, but most importantly I was determined to trust God with my whole soul.

I was still struggling with being alone. I had friends and family in my life, but I so desperately wanted someone with whom to share my life. I had always dreamt of having a husband some day that was kind, considerate, devoted, and loving. I was still working on giving everything to God and felt selfish praying for such a person. Ken was teaching me, however, that we can talk to God about anything, and that we need to give everything to Him. There is nothing wrong with opening up to God and sharing what we feel our hearts need. But, we need to understand how important it is to trust God's plan for our life, and that plan sometimes involves answered prayers and at other times unanswered prayers.

I had prayed throughout my life, but now I realized I was still learning how to open up to God, how to get close to Him, and how to trust Him completely. I always thought I had to pray a specific way, and that it was selfish to pray for things I felt my heart needed. But I was realizing we need to be close to God, and in order to get close to Him we have to learn to turn to Him for everything! How could a specific prayer fill those needs? Therefore, I started talking to God as if He was my best friend, and it felt great to open up my heart and be myself without having to perform a ritual of praying the same prayer over and over, which I felt I had to do in order to heal my soul. God sent Jesus to not only forgive our sins but also to help us understand that we need to be close to Him. We cannot let rituals prevent us from reaching Him. He wants us close to Him. He doesn't want rituals getting in the way of our relationship with Him. Each of us has a direct line to God through prayer, and we should use it frequently! My prayers were my personal, private conversations with God – only between God and me – so I really was able to open up my heart to Him.

I found myself praying often for God to bring a wonderful man into my life according to His will. For the first time I realized I trusted God completely, and so I gave Him my loneliness and sadness. I trusted His plan while I continued to struggle intermittently with feeling depressed. A short time later, God sent a great man into my life. It was as if God had filled my order perfectly and sent me a kind, compassionate soul in my husband Chris. He was very different from the other guys I had dated who seemed to be self-absorbed, caring more about themselves than others.

When I met Chris I was Catholic, so to later research and discover the story of Saint Christopher was incredible. Saint Christopher, whose name means "Christ carrier," was said to have carried Jesus on his back across the river, but the burden was so heavy it was almost too much to bear. The waters had big swells and continued to make the path difficult, especially while carrying such a heavy weight on his shoulders. It became so treacherous that he feared he might drown, but he pushed forward until he had the child Jesus on safe ground once again. When he asked the child why he weighed so much, He responded that He carries the world's sins on His shoulders. Christopher became known as the saint of travel or journeys to keep people safe.[2]

Although the story of Saint Christopher is not in the Bible, I have to wonder if it is a coincidence that the man brought into my life is also named Christopher. He was sent by God to keep me safe during the journey we would face together, and just like the burden Saint Christopher had to bear, my husband Chris would later carry a heavy burden on his own shoulders, a burden that would be too much for most people to bear. Although the journey included challenges most young married couples could not imagine facing, he kept pushing forward, carrying me through the storms I would not be strong enough to endure on my own. However, I was slowly discovering the secret to the same contagious peace and joy that radiated from Ken. This complete peace, which I longed to have myself, would be exactly what we needed to get through what was ahead.

CHAPTER 2

In Sickness and In Health

(Age 24)

Wilt thou have this Woman as thy wedded wife, to live together after God's ordinance in the holy state of Matrimony? Wilt thou love her, comfort her, honour, <u>and keep her in sickness and in health</u>; and, forsaking all others, keep thee only unto her, so long as ye both shall live?

When a couple marries under God, often their vows include "in sickness and in health." Chris and I had no idea that a few weeks after being married, we would be faced with the true meaning of those words and why they are such an important part of wedding vows.

Wedding Bells

"I can't believe it, the day is finally here!" I said to my sister as she was graciously helping me step into my wedding gown. A year and a half of planning for this day, and here it was! This was the day I'd dreamt about since I was a little girl – my wedding day. I had kissed my share of toads before I found an incredibly kind-hearted, compassionate man in my soon-to-be new husband Chris. The devotion and love he brought to our relationship was what fairy tales are made of, and he was certainly unlike any other guy I had dated.

"We have to hurry! The limo is going to be here in 15 minutes," my sister said as she was helping to button the endless row of buttons down the back of my dress. I peeked out the window and saw the rain still coming down. "Oh, can't I just catch a break for one day?" I said as I sighed. It seemed my life consisted of an infinite gray cloud hanging over my head. It had become a family joke that if anything could happen to anyone, it would happen to me. However, I had grown to understand that God only gives us what we can handle, so I knew to stay focused on the silver lining no matter how many clouds or storms surrounded me.

We gathered up the umbrellas and rushed out the door to where the limo was waiting. The rain actually let up to a light drizzle, so I was able to duck into the limo without getting drenched and ruining hours of preparation for our "perfect day." We arrived at the church and again scurried inside with umbrellas in tow. I was beginning to get nervous but my excited thoughts outweighed any nervous feelings. *What kind of life will we have? Will we be blessed with children? Will we be the rarity and proudly be able to celebrate our 50th wedding anniversary some day?* There was one thing I knew for certain, though: I was thankful God had sent me such an incredible man with whom to share my life. Chris has a compassionate soul, one you can sense just being around him. He is a great man whom I feel very blessed to have in my life.

The ceremony was powerful. I had no idea it would move me the way that it did. I had put so much focus on the reception, worrying about the perfect cake, music, and food, that I had lost sight of what was most important – the marriage ceremony. I was twenty-four years old at the time, so I had not yet experienced enough things in life to realize that none of those details mattered, and that what mattered was God bringing two people together to share their lives, to be there for each other, and to love each other through the good times and the bad. God knew how much I would need a caring, compassionate soul throughout the years, and He sent me a "one-in-a-million" guy in Chris to help me through them. We had no idea what was ahead but God knew, and He sent me an angel to be by my side every step of the way.

As we were pronounced husband and wife, I looked into my new husband's eyes, and in that moment both our eyes filled with tears as we silently shared big hopes for the future. He gave me a gentle squeeze with both hands letting me know he would be there for me. When the church doors opened for our departure, we saw that every cloud in the sky had disappeared. The sky was a beautiful blue without a trace of gray – what an incredible gift! It was as if God was shining down on us that very moment. We got into the limo after a few minutes of Chris picking up yards of satin from my wedding gown and gently tucking it inside so it wouldn't get caught in the door.

We were off to the reception and then scheduled early the next morning to board a plane to Florida for our honeymoon. I was so excited; we were going to Disney World!

CHAPTER 3

Weathering the Storm

(Age 24)

"Then they cried out to the Lord in their trouble, and he brought them out of their distress. He stilled the storm to a whisper; the waves of the sea were hushed. They were glad when it grew calm, and he guided them to their desired haven. Let them give thanks to the Lord for his unfailing love ..." (Psalm 107:28-31).

We had been in Florida five days and were enjoying a nice breakfast at a little café down the road from our hotel. As the waitress was placing our food on the table she said, "I've lived in Florida all of my life, and it has never rained five days in a row without a bit of sunshine." I smiled at my husband, shrugged my shoulders with a wry smile, and said, "Of course, the gray cloud followed me here and even took the sunshine out of the Sunshine State!" I chuckled and started to eat my breakfast because I knew there was a silver lining around every gray cloud.

We had decided we were not going to let the rain ruin our honeymoon. We set out to visit the main attractions as well as the water parks. The skies were filled with not an ounce of blue, only gray, but we decided we were going to enjoy our honeymoon and not let the weather spoil anything. We had a blast going down the water slides while it was pouring rain. We felt like we were kids again playing in the rain, jumping in mud puddles, expecting our parents to yell out the door to come in out of the rain, but we had a whole day to play in the puddles if we wanted to!

The day before we were to catch our flight home, we both caught horrible colds. We felt pretty miserable so we looked into flying back early, but the cost to change the flights wasn't worth it. Consequently, the last day of our honeymoon we snuggled up together in the hotel room watching movies and taking care of each other's sniffles. We were snuggled in bed surrounded by tissues and cups of warm tea. I look back and smile at the memory of that day, because despite the rain, the clouds, and the colds, we had a great time being together.

When we returned home, we went to the doctor and received antibiotics for the upper respiratory infections we had both contracted. I remember feeling really tired and thinking, *Wow, this is really taking a lot out of me.* I figured it was just the letdown of a year and a half of wedding planning, a rainy honeymoon, being sick, and trying to get back into the swing of things returning to the rat race at work. We were both starting to feel a little better and were excited we were now Mr. and Mrs.

About a week after I finished my antibiotic I noticed what appeared to be a strange rash on my legs. It hadn't been there that morning so I figured it must have been the new shaving lotion I had purchased the week before. When it didn't improve after a few days, I showed the rash to Sandie since she was like a mom to me and asked her if she had ever seen a rash like this, and she said, "No." She said I really should make an appointment to see a doctor, so I called the very next day.

After two hours of sitting in the waiting room, I finally saw the doctor. He examined me and said it looked like petechia.

"Peteaky what?" I said.

He repeated, "Petechia. It is a small purplish spot caused by a minute hemorrhage." I thought, *Hemorrhage? Why would I hemorrhage?* He saw the concerned look on my face and said, "No worries, it is probably just a reaction to the sulfa antibiotic you just finished. We'll run some blood work and see what we find." Off to the lab I went with multiple boxes checked under the blood part of the form and a typical scribbled doctor's signature across the bottom. They drew my blood and said it would take a few days for the results, so I was scheduled back the next week to see my doctor.

I hadn't given any more thought to it since the doctor said it was probably a reaction to the medicine, although the spots didn't improve. I started noticing them inside my mouth and even on my eyes. I left work early to follow up with the doctor on the day of my scheduled appointment. I flipped through an outdated *Family Journal* magazine while I waited. There were such adorable babies in the ads, and my mind drifted off imagining what our children would look like some day. *Will they have Chris' eyes? His smile? My laugh?* I just sat there smiling and feeling blessed for the new husband in my life. God was just too good to me. I was so excited at the thought of having a family of my own some day, and I trusted God would bless us with children. The nurse called me back and the doctor came in just a few minutes later.

"Sandi, have you been in a bad car accident or anything traumatic lately?" the doctor asked. I looked at him with a puzzled look; *what a bizarre question,* I thought.

"No, why?" I replied.

He said, "Well, your blood work came back a bit concerning. Your platelets were 10,000 and a normal range for an adult is between 150,000 – 300,000."

"Platelets? What are platelets?" I asked.

He replied, "They are a component of the blood that helps the blood to clot. Your counts are so low that you are at severe risk for hemorrhaging."

What? Did I hear him correctly? They must have my blood work confused with someone else's results. I am only twenty-four and just starting out my life ... there MUST be some mistake! This cannot be happening. God is good to me.

Suddenly, all of the images of what our babies' faces might look like were quickly replaced with worry about what all of this meant … *will I be able to have children? Is it Cancer? Will I die young?* Talk about having your life flash in front of your eyes. As I sat there looking dazed, the doctor explained what steps he would take next. "We're going to draw another blood count today to see if there was an error in the lab. I'll call you when the results are in." I thought, *phew that is exactly it, a lab error; there is nothing wrong with my blood counts.* Regardless, worry kept creeping into my mind along with the whole "What if?" scenario. I did my best to give it to God because I knew worrying certainly would not help my situation any, but this news was overwhelming. I prayed for strength.

CHAPTER 4

Waiting for the Call

(Age 24)

"Cast all your anxiety on Him because He cares for you"
(1 Peter 5:7).

"Sandi you have a call on line three, Sandi, line three," came the announcement over the work intercom. "Good morning, this is Sandi; may I help you?" I answered. It was the doctor himself, not the nurse – that was a bit startling. "Sandi, your platelet count is now down to 7,000, so there was not an error in the lab." *What? No, he must be mistaken. The blood count has to be wrong.* He said, "Hello, are you still there?" I was there but didn't know what to say; this was the last thing I had expected to hear.

He said he was referring me to see a hematologist and that I should hear from their office soon. I sat there in shock thinking, *what is a hematologist?* I called my husband right away to explain what the doctor had said. He sat there silent, too, but eventually said, "Don't worry, everything is going to be alright.

I am here for you. We will face this together. Focus on how healthy you are and how good you take care of yourself." *Yeah, he's right,* I thought – *I will be just fine; after all, I am healthy, I work out every day, and I am in my early twenties ...all will be fine.* Just the sound of his voice comforted me. I thanked God again for having Chris in my life.

A week later I went to my appointment with the hematologist, and while I waited for the doctor the nurse explained to me that a hematologist specializes in diseases of the blood. *Diseases?* I thought. The doctor came in and explained he was going to need to run some additional blood work and was ordering a bone marrow aspiration. *Oh my, this sounds serious – a bone marrow aspiration.*

"Do I have cancer?" I asked as my stomach dropped. It's one of the questions you don't want to hear the answer to, but still you have to ask. I stopped mid-breath waiting for his response. He said, "It is not clear yet what is causing your platelets to be so low, but that is what we are going to find out."

He scheduled the bone marrow aspiration for a week later and explained that I should have someone drive me. He said, "Since you are so young, it may be difficult to do the aspiration on the breastbone, but that is what I would like to try first because it is less painful than the hip." *Pain, oh my now this is sounding scary.* On the drive home I kept blinking my eyes so I could see to drive through the tears. I felt sad that Chris and I were just starting our life together and that within weeks of coming home from our honeymoon, we were being faced with what appeared to be a pretty major health issue – one that could forever change our lives. I prayed for strength to understand all that we were facing. I went home to call my family and update them with the news. Everyone was trying to stay positive, but I could tell they were as scared as I was.

The bone aspiration went well. The doctor was able to perform it on the breastbone so the pain was tolerable. I had heard stories about how painful the aspiration from the hip could be from other patients that had experienced it. I was thankful the doctor was able to avoid the hip area for me. It was uncomfortable, but not nearly as bad as I had expected it to be. It would take a week for the results. I was still trying to comprehend that just a few weeks ago I had just gotten married and was excited to start our new life together. Instead of worrying about how to decorate our new home or how we were going to get all of the thank-you notes written, we were worrying about the results of my next test and blood count. I kept reminding myself to focus on the silver lining no matter how big this gray cloud seemed.

I tossed and turned all night knowing that my doctor's appointment was tomorrow to review the results of the bone marrow aspiration. The waiting seemed like eternity but the day was finally here – now to just gather up enough courage to accept whatever the doctor had to say. While we sat in the waiting room, I flipped through magazines but could not focus on reading any of the articles because my mind was racing. *Jesus, please take this worry and anxiety from me,* I prayed silently. When we heard the nurse call my name, Chris and I walked back not knowing what we would hear and how it might change our lives. While we waited for the doctor to come in, Chris sat by me holding my hand and letting me know he was right by my side through it all. I gave him a forced smile and squeezed his hand. He knew I was being as strong as I could be, but it was difficult. I was struggling with giving it completely to God. I kept trying but couldn't seem to quite let go of all my worries and fears.

The doctor said the test came back with increased megacaryocytes; here was another medical term that meant nothing to us. He may as well have been talking to us in another language because we heard the word but had no idea what he was saying. He said the results of the bone marrow aspiration and a positive antibody against my platelets indicated that I had Idiopathic Thrombocytopenia Purpura, also known as ITP. Apparently, ITP is a rare blood disorder where the body develops an antibody against its platelets thus attacking them at dangerous levels. The doctor explained that there are a few treatments, but the first one typically involves surgically removing the spleen.

"Surgery? Why surgery?" I asked the doctor.

He responded patiently, "The last couple of months your body has failed to respond to the steroid treatment. By removing your spleen, there is a 50% chance your blood counts will go back to normal." I sat there overwhelmed at how scary just the thought of having surgery was to me. *Shouldn't you only have to have surgery if your appendix burst, or you get into some horrible accident? How is it at twenty-five I'm sitting here facing surgery, and just six short months ago I was on my honeymoon?* At that moment I realized that life is not a guarantee; it is a gift. I was learning to appreciate each day, whereas previously I had taken life for granted. I desperately wanted my normal life back.

I said to the doctor, "If it means I can get back to a normal life, then let's get this behind us." The doctor's office scheduled the pre-op visit and then surgery for a couple of weeks later.

~~~~~~~~~~

"I'm not sure. I can't find that much information at the library except a few medical definitions here and there. There isn't much information on ITP at all," I told my dad. Everyone had so many questions, but there weren't a lot of answers. My doctor found some articles for me to support the statistics regarding having my spleen removed. I needed something to share with my family, wanting to give them some hope that all would work out. I needed some hope as well.

"I am scared. The whole idea of surgery just petrifies me. You heard of that guy last year that went in for ankle surgery and died on the operating table? It seems like one horror story after another," I said to my husband. He put his arms around me and gave me a gentle hug to let me know he understood, and that he was there for me. I had no idea at the time just how much he would be there for me or how many more surgeries I would be facing over the upcoming years.

I found that the thoughts of surgery were overwhelming me not only at night when I tried to sleep, but during the day too. *What if I don't pull through the surgery? What about our future? I want a family ... I just want a normal life!* I screamed silently in my thoughts. *Is anyone listening? Does anyone care?*

My surgery was about a week away, and I was growing increasingly nervous. We were all anxious ... my husband, my dad, my mom, my sister and brother – everyone. It didn't help that they saw how anxious I was about the whole thing. I was at a point where I didn't know where to turn. I felt lost and scared.

It then hit me so strongly that I needed to pray, pray, and pray some more! It was as if a guardian angel was screaming those words into my ear. Everything in my being responded with *yes, that is it!* I knew I needed to work on giving all of my worries to God. He was the only one who could take away all of my anxiety. I have always had faith, and God was no stranger in my life, but I had felt so overwhelmed with what was happening that I'd been seeking comfort and answers everywhere except for where I should have been. I took some quiet time that evening and gave God my worries, desperately pleading with Him to help me find the peace I needed. I was scared.

My dad dropped in for a visit one day. It seemed he was dropping in a lot more often since my diagnosis. I could see the worry in his face knowing his firstborn was facing such health issues. I think he just needed to see for himself that I was okay versus simply taking my word for it over the phone. He told me on more than one occasion that if he could take it all and endure it himself, he would do so, because he didn't want me going through all of this. He is an incredible man of integrity, love, compassion, dependability, and strength. I'm blessed with two great parents whose hearts are filled with love and care for those around them, especially their children. My parents were divorced when I was young, but I always knew how much they loved us kids. I have a younger brother, Mike, and a sister, Susan, who are both great souls. God has blessed me with a wonderful family who really loves and supports one another. I kept assuring them that I trusted God's plan. It's not easy going through all of this, but I have to trust Him.

~~~~~~~~~~

"Wow, you seem all happy and chipper. I thought your surgery was just a few days away; did they cancel it?" my dad asked. My surgery indeed was a few days away, but I was no longer worried. "Yep, sure is. It's actually six days away, but I'm not worried anymore." My dad looked at me with a puzzled look – this coming from a girl who for the last week and a half had been doing her best to put on a smile to hide how scared she was about this surgery.

"Dad, I had this incredible dream. I know it sounds silly, but I feel as if I have already had the surgery and all was fine. I saw myself in a hospital gown being rolled into the operating room. Next thing I know, the surgery was over, and the doctor was examining my incisions. He lifted my gown, and I saw three small bandages on my stomach. There was one right under the middle of my rib cage, another directly under my left breast at the base of my rib and another at the bottom of my rib cage on the left side." I pointed to the areas on my stomach where the small bandages were in my dream, so he knew where I meant. "Then my doctor said everything went great, and that I was going to do just fine." I told him smiling, "Then I woke up, and since having that dream I am not scared at all. I can't explain it, but I know everything is going to go great – no need to worry."

He said, "Aren't dreams strange at times? Small bandages … hmmm. You know, the doctor told you that you would have about a six-inch incision down your side. But if that dream helped you feel better about things then that is great. I'm happy to see you back to your normal, positive self. Looks like my 'Miss Positive Mental Attitude' is back." In high school when awards were given at our sports banquets, I always seemed to bring home the "Miss Positive Mental Attitude" award. I had a few plaques Dad proudly displayed on his wall at home. He has told me since I was a little girl that God gave me an attitude like no other, because I seemed to have hope in difficult circumstances when most would not, and I've always tried to lift the spirits of those around me. And as far back as he could remember I've always tried to save the world. "That's my girl," he said as he kissed the top of my head.

Surgery was next week, so the dream helped me give my anxieties to God, and it reminded me that He is there for me. Although I have been a Christian for as long as I can remember, the one thing that keeps amazing me is that once we open our hearts and believe, God never fails to send us exactly what we need at the time we need it the most. The dream gave me the peace I so desperately needed to face surgery. It's as if God took my hand, walked with me into the future, and showed me what was going to happen (in detail). Although I was doing my best in giving my worries to God and failing miserably, He did not forsake me. He felt my struggle and stepped in to help me trust Him. The dream was so detailed and real that it removed my worries and instilled the peace He wanted for me ... the same peace He wants for each of us.

~~~~~~~~~~

This time He worked through a dream, but God works through all different avenues to let us know He is there for us. Many times He works through people. I know personally I feel blessed when He calls on me to help others. It fills my soul with such a great feeling, like what the flowers must feel when receiving rain after a long drought – giving to others and blessing them quenches the soul. It is important that we listen to any tug of our hearts, because that tug probably means someone needs our help.

Recently I had a heart tug to contact a friend I had not seen since high school. We had become friends in the first grade and remained friends all the way through to our senior year. I had a dream that he was going through some troubles and needed a friend. I had not talked with him in fifteen years but felt God tugging on my heart to call him.

I had no idea how to locate him so I went to the Internet hoping to obtain his email address. Thank goodness, I found it! I sent an email letting him know about my dream explaining that I felt he might be struggling with something. I told him that I knew it seemed a bit odd, since I hadn't talked with him in so long, but I felt strongly that I had to check on him. Within a couple of hours my phone rang, and it was him! He said he did not know what to say because he had been struggling with an upcoming divorce, his faith, and just everything in life! He really did need a friend. We talked awhile, and I explained that this is how God works and to know he was never alone. God tugs on our hearts, so listen! I was glad I did because I was able to help a friend in need.

Here is a neat little story that tells how a young man listened to the tug on his heart despite the chance someone could think he was crazy.

> A young man had been to Wednesday night Bible Study. The Pastor had talked about listening to God and obeying the Lord's voice. The young man couldn't help but wonder, *Does God still speak to people?*

After the service, he went out with some friends for coffee and pie, and they discussed the message. Several of the group talked about how God had led them in different ways. It was about ten o'clock when the young man started driving home. Sitting in his car before pulling out of the parking lot, he began to pray, "God ... If you still speak to people, speak to me. I will listen. I will do my best to obey."

As he drove down the main street of his town, he had the strangest thought: *Stop and buy a gallon of milk.* He shook his head and said out loud, "God is that you?" He didn't get a reply and so he started on toward home. But once again there came the thought: *Buy a gallon of milk.*

The young man thought about little Samuel in the Bible, and how he didn't recognize the voice, and so he ran to Eli. "Okay, God, in case that is you," the young man said, "I will buy the milk."

It didn't seem like too hard a test of obedience. He could always use the milk. He stopped at a convenience store and purchased the gallon of milk and started off toward home. As he passed Seventh Street, he again felt the urge: *Turn down that street.* "This is crazy," he thought, as he drove past the intersection.

Again he felt that he should turn down Seventh Street. At the next intersection he turned back and headed down Seventh. Half jokingly, he said out loud, "Okay, God, I will."

He drove several blocks, when suddenly, he felt like he should stop. He pulled over to the curb and looked around. He was in a semi-commercial area of town. It wasn't the best, but it wasn't the worst of neighborhoods either.

The businesses were closed and most of the houses looked dark like the people were already in bed. Again, he sensed something: *Go and give the milk to the people in the house across the street.*

The young man looked at the house. It was dark, and it looked like the people were either gone or they were already asleep. He started to open the door and then sat back in the car seat. "Lord, this is insane. Those people are asleep, and if I wake them up, they are going to be mad and I will look stupid."

Again, he felt like he should go and give the milk to the people in the house. Finally, he opened the door of his car. "Okay God, if this is you, I will go to the house, and I will give them the milk. If you want me to look like a crazy person, okay. I want to be obedient. I guess that will count for something. But if they don't answer right away, I'm out of here."

He walked across the street and rang the bell. He could hear some noise inside. A man's voice yelled out, "Who is it? What do you want?" Then the door opened before the young man could get away. A man was standing there in his jeans and T-shirt. He looked like he'd just gotten out of bed. He had a strange look on his face, and he didn't seem too happy to have some stranger standing on his doorstep. "What is it?" he asked. The young man thrust out the gallon of milk, "Here, I brought this to you." The man took the milk and rushed down a hallway speaking loudly in Spanish. Then from down the hall came a woman carrying the milk toward the kitchen. The man was following her holding a baby. The baby was crying.

The man had tears streaming down his face as he turned to his unexpected visitor. The man began speaking and half crying, "We were just praying. We had some big bills this month, and we ran out of money. We didn't have any milk for our baby. I was just praying and asking God to show me how to get some milk."

His wife in the kitchen called out, "I asked Him to send an angel with some milk. Are you an angel?"

The young man reached into his wallet and pulled out all the money he had with him and put it in the man's hand. He turned and walked back to his car with tears rolling down his cheeks. He knew that God still answers prayers and that God still speaks to His people.

- Author Unknown

God does still speak to His people. He speaks to us in many different ways – through dreams, tugs on our heart, and through other people, but we have to make sure we are listening!

~~~~~~~~~~~~

I remember waking up groggy from the surgery, blinking my eyes as I tried to focus on anything around me. I heard a nurse softly say to me, "You did fine, dear – you are going to be okay." *What? The surgery is done, just like that? Seems like a minute ago I was being wheeled into the operating room.* I stayed in recovery for a short while and then was wheeled to my room.

The nurses carefully transferred me to my assigned hospital bed. After I'd been settled in my room for a little while and the pain had subsided, the nurse came in and said, "Since you have such a low platelet count, I need to check your dressings, honey." She lifted my gown, and when I looked at my abdomen my jaw dropped open … there on my stomach were three white bandages right where I had dreamt they would be. The doctor came into my hospital room to follow up and said the surgery went great! He shared with us that he had performed the first laparoscopic splenectomy at that hospital which only required three small incisions instead of the six-inch incision that we were all expecting. I was in awe once again at God and the ways He uses to reach us. I prayed and thanked Him for the dream He had sent me the week before. He knew just what I needed to get through this, and He had sent that message to me in a way He knew I would listen – a way that I would know was undeniably Him.

CHAPTER 5

Trusting God's Plan

(Age 25)

"Surely God is my salvation; I will trust and not be afraid. The Lord, the Lord, is my strength and my song; he has become my salvation" (Isaiah 12:2).

A Much Needed Getaway

"Cancun? We're really going to Cancun?" I jumped up and down like a kid who just got her favorite toy at Christmas. I was excited about the news my husband had just shared. He had booked a week-long vacation in Cancun at a five-star hotel, right on the ocean. "I thought we should try the honeymoon thing again since the first one was rained out. I don't think your gray cloud will follow us all the way to Mexico," he said as he smiled.

"This is great! I cannot wait, honey! You're the best!" I said to him as I squeezed him tightly and reached up to kiss him. He is 6'3" and towers over my barely 5'2" height.

As a little girl, I had dreamt of one day being able to go on a vacation like this. Growing up, we could not afford much. As a result, I had not taken many vacations in my life despite all of my friends heading off to somewhere fun every spring break. My parents divorced when I was eleven years old. My Dad had remarried a woman with three children of her own. He worked very hard, but supporting a family of six children left little room for any kind of luxuries. I always wished we could go on vacations and have nice clothes like other kids but God gave me what I needed. He blessed me with two parents that loved us unconditionally. Growing up this way also taught me to appreciate the simple things in life and helped me to understand that we don't *need* all of those luxuries to be happy.

Now, as an adult, I felt thankful for the blessings God was sending my way even if they were mixed with challenges. By now Chris and I had been married a couple of years. We had our share of challenges with my health during that time, but my body adjusted to surviving with a low platelet count. I failed every treatment and so I was diagnosed with what they call chronic refractory ITP. It meant constant visits to the doctor and repeated blood counts to monitor my platelets, but I did not let it control me, I focused on all of my blessings instead. Although I should have had some type of internal bleeding due to my low platelet count (which averaged around 15,000), I did just fine. I worked a normal schedule, continued to exercise at the health club, and lived a fairly normal life. Going to the lab to have blood counts just became part of my life. I decided that

I could either let this disease control me, or I could show it that I had God on my side!

"Don't forget to pack extra swim trunks and something nice to wear out in the evenings," I yelled to my husband while I was packing my suitcase. We had planned on spending our days sipping drinks by the poolside, and then going to nice dinners and dancing in the evenings. We were still newlyweds so we couldn't wait to escape to our romantic paradise. The doctors approved our vacation plans and were happy to see I wasn't letting this disease get me down.

We arrived at our hotel, and I had never seen a view as beautiful as the view from our 10th floor hotel room that overlooked the white sands and aqua water. "It is just beautiful," I said as my husband walked out onto the patio and hugged me from behind. I looked up and over my shoulder at him and said, "Thanks for doing this, it is just what I needed." He smiled and gently kissed the top of my head. *I am so blessed to have him in my life,* I thought happily as I gazed out at the paradise surrounding us. *He has been such an incredible support for me during these first couple of years. This situation would be difficult for most, and I am so blessed with a guy who has stayed by my side every step of the way.*

"Are you almost ready, Dear? I am starving, and you have been in there for almost an hour," Chris said patiently sitting on the patio waiting for me to finally be ready to go out. "Almost… I'll be out in a minute!" I yelled from the bathroom while I finished putting on my mascara. We headed out for our first night in Cancun. We went to a very romantic dinner where we ate by candlelight and enjoyed the authentic Mexican food we both love so much. We sipped champagne and discussed where we would go dancing that night. I yawned and said, "Wow, I am really tired. The sun took a lot out of me today. Would it be okay if we went back to the room tonight and went to bed early?" He looked at me with a strange expression, because I was always ready to go, especially when anything fun was involved. He said, "Of course, let's relax tonight if you're tired. We can go out tomorrow night." He was always understanding and caring. We went back to the room, and I was asleep by 9 o'clock.

Well, one night turned into six nights of me falling asleep early, and we didn't have one night out past dinner. Unfortunately for my husband this hadn't turned out to be much of a second honeymoon because his wife kept nodding off as soon as the sun was setting. I kept thinking it must be the sun and heat making me so tired.

Once we arrived back at home and had unpacked our suitcases, I was so exhausted and told my husband I was going to lie down to rest. He said, "Maybe you should call and get an earlier appointment at the doctor, because this is not like you to be so tired all of the time." *He is right. I will call to move up my appointment,* I thought as I drifted off to sleep.

My appointment was set for next week. My sister had called me at work to see how the vacation had gone. I mentioned to her how I had fallen asleep early every night. She asked, "Are you pregnant?"

I said, "What?"

She replied, "You said you have been really tired and falling asleep early every night. That's a good sign!" I thought, *nah I couldn't be pregnant ... could I?* She said, "You should pick up a pregnancy test; what harm would it do?" She was right, so I picked one up on my way home from work that day. I hadn't said anything to my husband because I was sure there was no way I was pregnant. Certainly the traveling and the heat and sun in Mexico must've taken a lot out of me.

After dinner I told my husband, I would be back downstairs in a minute. He sat on the couch with his feet propped up on the coffee table to relax and watch a little TV. We had always talked about how much we wanted a family but with everything going on with my health, we felt we needed to wait. I took the test and walked into the bedroom to change into something comfortable. I walked back into the bathroom and couldn't believe what I was seeing. *Is that a blue line in the pregnancy window? Oh my goodness, it was very blue not even a faint blue.* I read the instructions over and over again, double-checking and checking again. There was no mistake – there was a blue line, darker than ever in the pregnancy window of the test.

"Honey, could you come up here for a minute?" I yelled down the stairs to him in the family room. Although we thought we needed to wait to start our family because there were so many risks involved with my health condition, God obviously had different plans. I was flooded with all kinds of emotions… excitement, happiness, and fear! With the pregnancy test in my hand, I stood there shaking with tears in my eyes … I was pregnant!

> *"For I know the plans I have for you," declares the Lord, "plans to prosper you and not to harm you, plans to give you hope and a future. Then you will call upon me and come and pray to me, and I will listen to you. You will seek me and find me when you seek me with all your heart" (Jeremiah 29:11-13).*

CHAPTER 6

Unanswered Prayers

(Age 26)

"Trust in the Lord with all your heart and lean not on your own understanding; in all your ways acknowledge Him, and He will make your paths straight" (Proverbs 3:5-6).

"A little over a month to go before my first grandchild will be born," my dad said with a smile. Although everyone was very happy to hear the news that we were pregnant, the reaction was a mixture of complete excitement and worry due to my health situation. This would be the first grandchild on both sides of the family so everyone was nervous, but of course they tried not to show it around us.

"Honey, could you please put the crib over on that wall?" I asked my husband as I pointed to the south wall of the baby's bedroom while gently rubbing my very round, pregnant belly with my other hand. He looked at me and smiled, but I could tell he was trying to be as patient as possible because I kept changing my mind as to where exactly I wanted the crib placed.

"That looks great; it is just perfect. Thank you!" I said with a big smile after he muscled it over to the same wall he had placed it on originally. We did not want to know the sex of the baby, so we decorated the room a beautiful aqua green with a cheery, bright balloon design. The crib was filled with stuffed animals and the dresser was full of onesies, blankets, hooded bath towels, and diapers, all generous gifts from our baby shower the week before.

"Oh, look at the time. I have my doctor's appointment in thirty minutes," I said as I straightened the pillow in the rocking chair we received as a gift from my family. The doctor said it was time for me to start having weekly visits from now until the end of the pregnancy just so he could more closely monitor the baby and me, of course.

My platelet counts remained low throughout the entire pregnancy despite multiple prayers from family, friends, and local churches. I was given treatments of prednisone and IV Gamma Globulin the last few months in hopes of bringing my platelets up, but my counts would not budge. My average platelet count remained around 20,000. It seemed that with every low-platelet blood count new worries would find their way into our minds. It had been a long 35 weeks of worrying and doctor visits. However, we were on the home stretch now, with only five weeks to go – we were going to have a baby!

"Everything looks really good with both you and the baby. It's an exciting time, but you need to determine the date you want your baby to be born," Dr. Richman said. I knew I would need a C-Section to ensure the safest delivery for the baby and for my health, but I still had not become comfortable with the idea of picking the day our baby would be born. Isn't that part of the excitement – not knowing the day God is going to bless you with your brand-new baby?

I told my doctor, "We'd like to have a week to think about it, if that is okay. We can tell you what we decide during my next visit," I said as I carefully inched off of the examining table using my hands to keep my balance and ensuring my feet were securely planted on the floor. "No problem; I'll plan on seeing you next week, and we will get the C-Section scheduled. We will also do the amniocentesis test to ensure the baby's lungs are developed," said Dr. Richman.

I called my mother-in-law when I got home to update her of my latest visit. Everyone wanted a weekly update on how the grandbaby was doing. "Are you sure you want to go to the next visit by yourself? I think someone should come with you," she said. "No, I will be fine. I have been going every week by myself, so I'll be fine." She insisted on coming and wouldn't take no for an answer. I would soon realize what mother's intuition was all about and was very thankful she insisted on going to that visit with me.

~~~~~~~~~~

"Ready to go?" my mother-in-law asked. She was right on time to pick me up for my 36-week appointment. We arrived at the doctor's office a little early. We patiently waited to be called back so we could get the amniocentesis test started. I had to do my routine urine test, blood pressure, etc., and then the nurse got me settled into a room. The doctor came in to see me. After he examined me he said, "You need to call your husband because we are having the baby today." I looked at him surprised and said, "What?" I wasn't sure I'd heard him correctly. "You have developed pre-eclampsia. We need to deliver the baby soon to ensure that you and the baby are okay. Call your husband – it is time to have this baby," he said with a smile. We were struggling with deciding what day the baby was going to be born so God took things into His own hands and decided for us. What a gift!

I called my husband at work to tell him the news. "We're what?" he said in shock on the phone. "We are having the baby, so get to the hospital as soon as possible," I said into the receiver. He dropped everything and rushed to the hospital. Although we were having a C-Section, we still had the excitement of an unexpected delivery date. We were so very thankful for that. Who would have guessed it would turn out this way? I called my mom all excited to tell her we were having the baby TODAY! She lived out of state but today was her birthday, so she was more than excited that her first grandchild was going to share her birthday.

My husband arrived just in time to spend a few minutes with me, and then they were rolling me off to the operating room. He kept holding onto my hand and didn't want to let go. I saw the worry in his face. The doctor gently removed my husband's hand from mine, patted him on the back, and said with a reassuring smile, "She will be just fine, both her and the baby. I will come out as soon as the baby is born to give you an update."

My husband couldn't come into the operating room because I was a high-risk patient. He nervously waited in the waiting room with his parents and mine. They said it would be a little while so everyone insisted on going to the cafeteria to grab a quick bite for lunch. My husband didn't want to go, but they insisted he got something in his stomach. After being down there about a half an hour he said, "I will see you guys later. I have to get back up there." His mom said to him, "Now honey, I know you are nervous, but all will be fine. Just sit and eat a bit more, and then we will all go up soon." He felt strongly that he needed to go. "I'm sorry Mom, but I feel I need to get back up there. I can't explain it. I will plan on seeing you guys upstairs," he said as he gave her a hug and kiss on the cheek.

My husband walked down the long hallway and maze of turns on his way to the elevator. Who knows why cafeterias are so tucked away in some of these hospitals. As he was turning towards the elevator he met up with a nurse pushing a brand-new baby in a carrier with a plastic dome-like top towards the elevator. He did a double take at the nametag on the side of the carrier. Was he seeing the name correctly? He leaned in to look more closely and there scribbled in black letters on a blue nametag was our last name ...

RAUWOLF

His eyes got big, and he said excitedly, "That's my son!!" The nurse said smiling, "Well, congratulations, Dad, you have a healthy baby boy!" She explained to Chris that she was taking him up to the nursery. "Is there any chance I could go with you?" he said. She looked at him smiling and said, "Absolutely!"

He got on the elevator first, so he could hold the doors open while she maneuvered the baby carrier into the elevator. Chris couldn't keep his eyes off of the baby. The nurse had been in the delivery room, so she knew he had not been able to share in the experience of the live birth. She smiled as she lifted the case letting my husband reach his hand into the dome. He gently took his newborn son's tiny hand in his to hold. The love and bond were instant. Tears filled his eyes as he thanked God for this wonderful little miracle. He stood in awe at the perfect timing of them meeting in the hallway. *What a blessing being able to see my son when he's just minutes old,* he thought to himself as he wiped a tear from his cheek. It was the closest thing to being part of the delivery as possible. "Thank you God, for this incredible gift," he whispered under his breath.

Years later we found out that if God had answered everyone's prayers and brought my platelets to normal levels, we would have lost the pregnancy. The low count thinned my blood enough for the blood to flow to the baby, thus nurturing him in the womb. The clotting issues I had were not diagnosed until years later. At the time of the pregnancy, we did not realize what would have happened if the platelets had increased. A normal platelet count with clotting issues like mine would have stopped the blood flow to the baby causing spontaneous abortion. This was a valuable lesson in our spiritual journey teaching us to trust God's way even when we don't understand it. We were thankful for unanswered prayers and the miracle of our son's birth. Despite the odds, Tyler came into this world healthy and perfect. What an incredible blessing. We had a bouncing baby boy!

CHAPTER 7

Test of Faith

(Age 30)

"Have I not commanded you? Be strong and courageous. Do not be terrified; do not be discouraged, for the LORD your God will be with you wherever you go" (Joshua 1:9).

"I can't believe Tyler is turning four in a couple of weeks," I said to Chris as we lay next to each other in bed. A tear started running down my face. I thought to myself, *we had three years of a close to normal life after Tyler was born. I wouldn't trade those years for anything in this world.* I had gone into spontaneous remission shortly after his birth, yet another one of God's blessings. My mind flashed back to when I used to hold this little, precious angel and gently rock him during his feedings in the middle of the night. During those quiet, special moments, I would pray so intensely with tears streaming down my face asking God to hear my prayer. I prayed for it to be His will to make me well enough, even just for a few short years.

"Please, Jesus, give me a chance to be a mom and to enjoy the miracle you have blessed us with."

The thought of those times flooded me with emotion. It was as if I had gone back in time and was reliving it all over again. I thought, *Thank you, thank you so much for those years. You really did answer my prayers, and I am very thankful.* I had gone into remission in 1995 and was in remission until March of 1998, quite an incredible gift!

We faced other challenges during those few years but not due to my blood disorder. I had two miscarriages, one in 1995 and another in 1996. It was extremely difficult to go through. We didn't quite understand the pain felt by parents who'd lost a baby through miscarriage until we experienced it ourselves. We had no clue just how much we could love or miss a baby that we never even knew physically, but that did not matter because we still held them in our hearts so closely. It doesn't matter how far along the pregnancy was, they were still our babies.

The second miscarriage was harder than the first because we began to wonder if we would ever be able to have another child. I personally wouldn't let go of the thought because my heart felt like our family wasn't quite complete. Chris kept assuring me that my health was more important than having a second child, and he also kept reminding me that we had been more than blessed with Tyler. He was right, and I was grateful for our baby boy, but there was still this hole in my heart. I struggled with that constantly, but I learned to ask God to help us trust Him with His plan for us. It is not always easy to trust

Him, especially when being faced with things that just don't make sense, at least to us. I finally came to a place in life where I trusted God had a plan. Some day in God's time, not ours, if we were meant to grow our family, we would. My perspective began to change, and I realized that each miscarriage was a reminder to count our blessings, particularly one very special one named Tyler. We thanked God for him every day.

Chris looked at me and saw the tears rolling down my face. He put has arms around me, gently kissed my forehead and softly stroked my hair with a look that said, "I know honey, I know." He knew exactly what I was thinking: my health was doing well and life was better than great with our new son. We felt very blessed. I was very focused on staying healthy, so I worked out every day and watched what I ate, and I really felt terrific. But, as is common with many women, I was not happy with myself – no weight ever seemed good enough. I wanted to lose just five more pounds. Chris kept insisting that I looked great and told me frequently that I didn't need to lose any more weight. I didn't listen and kept doing everything possible to lose those last five pounds, which would not budge – it was so frustrating! I heard about a supplement that would help boost metabolism resulting in stubborn weight loss. I started taking it and within one month my blood counts crashed to dangerous levels. I put myself into the worst health spin I had experienced yet in my life – all to lose a few pounds.

I just began to sob thinking about it. I said, "Chris, how could I have been so stupid?!" He just hugged me and let me cry, assuring me it was okay. I don't know what I would do without those strong shoulders there for me. "Ty's fourth birthday is in a couple of weeks, and I am so sick I can barely get out of bed," I said to him as I cried harder.

The last year had consisted of constant trips to the hospital, often in the middle of the night. I was put on multiple medications and treatments, all of which were failing miserably. We were at a point where no new treatments or options were available for my disorder – every treatment had failed. The thought was discouraging, so I kept turning to God for my strength.

During my pregnancy with Tyler, I became anemic and was later diagnosed with Evans Syndrome (a combination of ITP and Hemolytic Anemia). My blood counts were critical and that included both my platelets and red blood cells. The red blood cells carry oxygen through your body. Since mine were critical, I had a difficult time trying to breathe. Any simple exertion was a major effort for me. I was also severely jaundiced. My skin and eyes were very yellow as a result of my body killing off red cells so fast that my liver couldn't keep up with filtering all of it out of my blood. The treatments were only making things worse for my liver which intensified things. I had horrible side effects from all of the drugs I was on. I became hypertensive (high blood pressure), developed steroid-induced diabetes, not to mention the famous steroid moon face. The prednisone caused my face to swell so much it was as if I was wearing a fat suit. It also caused me to gain a lot of weight. I had gained 40 pounds in three months' time and had gone from a size 6 to a size 14. The added weight caused more health issues for me not to mention all of the other side effects from the multiple drugs. At times I was taking in excess of 70 pills a day.

I was quickly realizing that not only was every day a gift, but every minute as well. I did my best to focus on all of the blessings in my life and not on all of the challenges. There I sat, thirty years old with a beautiful family, wishing I could feel well enough to be a good mom and a good wife, but knowing just walking to the bathroom was a major effort. I felt as if I was becoming a blood junkie, since blood transfusions were my fix to feeling well, even if only for a few hours. The blood gave me life. It provided the red blood cells I needed for the oxygen to be supplied to my body. Yes, I knew it was short-lived and only a matter of hours before my body would kill the new cells, but at least it would give me some time of feeling like I could breathe a little easier. It would give me a little energy to hug my son and read a book to him. I was thankful God tugged at the hearts of those people who would never meet me but so unselfishly gave me, a young wife and mother, a gift, a very important one ... the gift of life by donating blood.[3]

Oddly enough, however, it seemed that with each transfusion, my body's attack on my blood cells became more and more aggressive. "God, I know you are there – please hear my prayers. Please help me through this, but more importantly, help my family to find the strength and faith You have blessed me with. They need that faith more than they realize. It will help them understand how important it is for us to trust in Your plan, especially when we don't understand it."

As in the poem *Footprints*, I found myself turning more and more to God, particularly when I was not strong enough to endure things on my own.

Footprints in the Sand

One night I dreamed I was walking along the beach
with the Lord. Many scenes from my life flashed
across the sky. In each scene I noticed footprints in
the sand. Sometimes there were two sets of footprints,
other times there were one set of footprints.

This bothered me because I noticed that during the low
periods of my life, when I was suffering from anguish,
sorrow or defeat, I could see only one set of footprints.

So I said to the Lord, "You promised me Lord,
that if I followed you, you would walk with me
always. But I have noticed that during the most
trying periods of my life there have only been one
set of footprints in the sand. Why, when I needed
you most, you have not been there for me?"

The Lord replied, "The times when you have seen only
one set of footprints in the sand, is when I carried you."[4]

- Mary Stevenson

CHAPTER 8

The Best Christmas Gift

(Age 30)

"Call to me and I will answer you and tell you great and unsearchable things you do not know" (Jeremiah 33:3).

"Honey, I can't believe it is Christmas Eve, and I am in the hospital. I want to be home with you and Tyler. I don't want to be here, I just want to go home," I said to Chris as tears welled up in my eyes. He gently squeezed my hand and looked at me. He always tried to be strong for me, but I could see all of the pain in his face. I trusted God with His plans for my life, but it was difficult seeing the pain on the faces of those who loved me so much. Tyler wasn't old enough to understand what was going on, but he sensed something was wrong because his mom and dad seemed to always be at the hospital, especially around the holidays. I had spent Thanksgiving that year in the hospital and now, at Christmas, I found myself in the hospital again.

This hospital visit was different, though. The last few weeks I had progressively become worse. My stomach was extremely swollen. I had what they called abdominal distention. I felt and looked like the blueberry girl from the famous kid's book and movie called *Charlie and the Chocolate Factory*. The only difference was I didn't have a golden ticket! Instead I'd had severe pain in my abdomen for the last month. Nothing would take the pain away. I could not get complete relief from anything. The only thing that would help ease the pain a little bit was a hot bath. I would find myself taking up to three baths in the middle of the night and praying for a few minutes of relief from the relentless pain. Test after test had shown there was no blockage and nothing wrong, but I knew intuitively that something was wrong. Something was really wrong! My counts were very low, so much that I couldn't take a couple of steps without being out of breath. I didn't have enough red cells to carry oxygen through my body. Having a thirty-year-old soul in what felt like a hundred-year-old body was difficult, at best.

I had an incredible doctor who had followed my case for some time. Despite my having a rare, challenging blood disease, he continued to care for me with any treatment available for my condition. He always encouraged me through his kindness and incredible bedside manner to hold onto hope and keep my positive outlook despite how discouraging the medical condition was that our young family was facing. He never discussed faith in God with me, but I sensed – without a doubt – that God was working through him even without words being exchanged.

God also seemed to be working through one particular nurse named Heather. She had worked with my doctor for years, and it always seemed that just when I needed her most she was assigned to take care of me during my hospitalizations. She would come in and sit with me to talk and listen to me, offering me encouragement, compassion, and incredible care. She later told me she couldn't explain how during each of my hospital visits something had guided her to check the patient registry, and there she would find my name. Even when she wasn't assigned to take care of me, she would come and see me just to sit and talk with me, to "care for me" more than she realized. She would even show up to be with my family before any surgery or procedure I was about to go through. We loved her; she was like an angel, and I believe one of many earth angels that God sent our way.

~~~~~~~~~~

My doctor had ordered a special abdominal CT scan earlier that day, so I lay in my hospital bed anxiously waiting that appointment. I had to drink contrast liquid to prepare for the test, as it would allow the imaging to pick up all of the details, hopefully providing some answers as to what could be causing all of this pain and distention in my abdomen. The chalky liquid was in two large containers, and I wanted to cry at the thought of drinking them. I could barely drink a sip of water; how would I drink all of this? I knew how important it was, so I prayed I could get it all down somehow.

No matter how much I tried, I just couldn't drink it all. It took me twice as long as instructed to drink one container. I could not drink the other. I sat there discouraged with tears rolling down my face. I had to get this test done if I had any hope at all of going home to be with my son for Christmas. And, after all of this effort, I wasn't sure if the test would even show the proper results, since I wasn't able to drink it all. I prayed, "Jesus, please hear my prayers and get me through this!" Every passing minute the thought kept creeping into my mind that this could be the last Christmas I would get to spend with my family. I had never felt this ill before.

Despite not being able to drink the remainder of that horrible, chalky concoction, they placed me in a wheelchair and pushed me downstairs to the radiology department of the hospital for the abdominal CT scan. The ride seemed like it took forever. Sitting there, even without any exertion on my part, I felt very sick. No matter how deeply I tried to breathe, I just couldn't get enough oxygen into my lungs or my body. The only way I can think to describe it is that I felt like a desperate goldfish gasping to fill its lungs with life-giving oxygen, but no matter how deeply it attempts to breathe, it is hopeless.

I was a fish out of water.

It was difficult, but the technician helped me get onto the scanning table. He connected the radioactive tube to my IV and started to slowly inject the dye. I felt this warm sensation go throughout my body as the dye filled my circulatory system. I lay there as the machine slowly guided me into the CT tube opening and I heard the machine announce, "Hold your breath ... Now breathe." I prayed that enough contrast liquid was in my abdomen for the doctors to see what they needed to see. The technician proudly announced that he was able to get the pictures and the images looked good! The test was behind me now. Thank God for that! As I was pushed back to my room, I knew I had to convince my doctors somehow to let me go home to spend Christmas with my family. My doctor came to check on me shortly after I arrived back into my room.

"Sandi, it is obvious you are not feeling well and your counts are very low. It is not advisable to release you," the doctor said with a great deal of concern in his voice. My husband sat next to me already distraught, so I didn't want to say anything more to upset him. However, I had to somehow let the doctor know that I desperately NEEDED to be home because I sensed this was my last holiday. I didn't want to spend it in the hospital away from my family. I continued to plead with him while I silently prayed that God would help me get my message across and get me where I needed to be. "But doctor, I am willing to take that risk. Being home with my son Christmas morning is all I want right now. I already feel very ill ... please just let me go home to have Christmas morning with him, even if I have to come right back again." He was a father, and I could tell he understood what I was trying to share with him. He agreed that if the initial scan results came back okay, then he would allow me to go home that Christmas Eve. I was thankful for his consideration. I was torn because I knew I was too sick to leave, but I also knew, with every fiber in my being, that I couldn't be apart from Chris and Tyler that Christmas.

I lay in my hospital bed watching the time tick by. It was almost 5 o'clock on Christmas Eve, and I was still waiting for the results from the CT scan. "Chris, I will be devastated if I can't go home tonight. I miss Tyler so desperately and with everything I have been through, I just want Christmas morning together with you and him. Do you think God will give that to me?" I sat there crying and praying for God to hear me. I am sure God was getting real tired of hearing all of my desperate pleas, or was He? My husband hugged me and held me so close to him. He felt the pain I was going through.

When you get married, in God's eyes you become one, and during those moments my husband felt the pain of every single tear with me, and I found myself often overwhelmed with what all of this was doing to him. The phrase "in sickness and in health" seems like mere words, but when you find yourself living them, they hold new meaning. This incredible man did not deserve the pain my health issues were burdening his heart with. God somehow gave me the continued strength to face my ordeal, but to sit and watch it devastate this incredible "one-in-a-million" man, whom I loved, was hard.

My doctor walked into my room. "The initial results are in and nothing specific is showing so I am going to release you to go home and spend Christmas morning with your family," the doctor said as he smiled. I knew what a gift he had just given me. I held my arms out to hug him and say, "Thank you so much for this very special gift. God bless you!" My husband quickly gathered my stuff together and pulled the car around while an orderly pushed me to the front of the hospital so they could load me into the car. I was scared leaving the hospital, and I could sense my husband was scared as well because he knew how sick I was. I knew I should not be going home, but the love I had for my family and my need to be with them for this one last holiday was so strong that I would risk anything and everything for that opportunity. There was no other choice for me. I just felt it.

The ride back was grueling; with every small bump in the road a sharp pain would shoot through my abdomen. I sat with a bucket on my lap in case I got sick, and I was just praying we could get home soon. I lay my head back on the headrest of the car seat feeling sicker by the minute. *Please, God, just get us home and get me in bed.* Every minute became a bigger challenge to breathe. Then a jolting thought struck me! *I have been so focused on Christmas morning, but what if I'm not well enough to even make it through the night? No, I have to stop that kind of thinking and trust God. I will pray and have faith that He will give me this last gift of being with my family tomorrow morning.*

Finally, one more turn and we would be in our driveway. The thirty-minute ride seemed to have taken hours, but we were finally home, thank goodness! I opened my car door and tried to step out despite Chris' pleas to sit tight so that he could come around to my side of the car and help me. I have always been too independent for my own good. I took one step and almost fell. I didn't have any energy at all. The ride took everything out of me. My husband was there to grab me. (He had long since learned to be one step ahead of me.) I was so thankful for him. Yet again he was there to catch me when I stubbornly tried to do something I shouldn't have done and was about to fall. He gently picked me up and carried me into the house and straight up to bed. I lay there feeling so thankful to be home and continued to pray that God would get me through the night. I just kept smiling in anticipation of seeing Tyler's face Christmas morning as he beamed with excitement over what Santa had left under the tree for him. Those kinds of moments were like no other ... despite the circumstances, what a gift the doctor had given me by allowing me to go home for this chance to be with my family.

I finally drifted off to sleep, and it didn't seem like long before Tyler was at our bedside pulling on our covers saying, "Mom, Dad ... Santa came! Santa came! Come and see!!!" He was a very excited little four-year-old! My husband told him to go and sit by the tree, and we would be right down. I was too weak to walk, so my husband carried me downstairs and sat me on the couch right next to the Christmas tree where Tyler was running around checking out each package as if he knew how to read each tag.

Again, I was thankful for this gift on Christmas morning, and I don't mean the packages under the tree! Tyler tore through packages with a vengeance. His favorite gift that year from Santa was a toy guitar with a shoulder strap. It came with a microphone on a stand, just like a real music star would use. He loved music and loved being on center stage even more! His favorite song was "Greased Lightning." We put in the CD and watched him play his pretend guitar with gusto and sing boisterously into the microphone. He kept stopping and coming over to hug me as if he knew how important this was to all of us. Despite his arms being so little, each hug felt like I was being surrounded by the love of a giant. *Thank you, God – Thank you so much for this Christmas gift,* I thought.

We watched Ty play until almost lunchtime. Since I was very ill, our families changed all of their Christmas plans at the last minute and decided to bring the food and gifts from their homes to ours so we could spend the holiday together. We are blessed with a great family!

About the time everyone was to arrive, I felt my time was coming and I was growing weaker by the moment. I couldn't bring myself to say that to Chris, but I felt with everything in me that this was it, and I needed to get up to bed to be alone and pray. "Chris, I am not feeling very well and want to lie down awhile. Would you please take me up to bed?" I asked him. "Ty, come give Mommy a big hug and kiss, I am going to go rest a bit. I love you so very much, peanut!!" I said to him. He ran over with the toy guitar still strapped over his shoulder and gave me the best hug and kiss! I hugged him so tightly and did not want to let go, EVER! I had to look away because tears were filling my eyes. I didn't want him to see me upset or know what my mind was thinking, which was *what if this is the last time I get to hug my baby?*

Chris carried me upstairs and got me settled into bed. I gave him a gentle, loving hug and told him how very much I loved him as I kissed him. I asked him to please close the door behind him. The moment the door shut, I began to pray harder than I had ever prayed before. "Jesus, I trust your plan for me and am praying for the strength to endure all that I am facing right now. Thank you for this incredible gift of being with my family this Christmas morning. But, I have yet another prayer. I am very ill and need a miracle! I can feel with each minute that I am becoming weaker. If now is not my time, and you will bless me with another chance, please hear my prayers and send me a miracle. Amen."

At that time, I closed my eyes and waited patiently to see if my prayers would be answered. It was about 1 o'clock in the afternoon, and at that moment our phone rang. I figured it was someone in our family letting us know they were on their way, as well as checking in to see how I was doing. I heard footsteps running up the stairs and then suddenly the door was quickly opened and my husband was standing there with an urgent look on his face. "Honey, it is the doctor, and he wants to talk to you right away," Chris said. I looked at him puzzled; the doctor was calling me on Christmas day? I took the phone and hesitantly said "Hi, doctor … this is Sandi …"

"Sandi, I just received a call from the hospital, and I do not know what made the senior radiologist pick up your films out of 150 films, but he did. He found clots going to your major organs. You need to get to the hospital *right now*," my doctor said. I dropped the phone and yelled for Chris, oblivious that he was still standing right there in front of me waiting to hear what the doctor had to say. "We have to go to the hospital right now!" I quickly explained what the doctor had just shared.

The family began filtering in the bedroom door while Chris was gathering me from bed. He yelled to them the news from the doctor and that we had to go NOW to the hospital. We hugged and kissed them all as he grabbed me, blanket and all, to place me in the car. As we were going out the door, Tyler ran over to me and wrapped his arms around my neck tight with so much love that it radiated throughout my soul.

As Chris was rushing me to the car, I looked back and saw Tyler standing in the slightly steamed glass door with big tears in his eyes. His little hands were on the glass of the door as if he was trying to reach through the door to get to me. He had a sad look that said, "Mommy, please don't leave me." I reached my hand out to him sobbing and hoping somehow he would know how very much I loved him and how I never wanted to leave him.

I didn't realize at the time that this was very symbolic of how God must feel when we are trying to reach out to Him, and how sad He must be when there is something between us and Him. We can still see Him, but the glass door, which is often our sin, keeps us from being close to Him. It blocks us, not from knowing He is there but from being close to Him until we open our hearts to Jesus. And when we do, the forgiveness of our sins opens the door, allowing us who are God's children to be close to Him again, just as Tyler so desperately wanted to be close to me that cold Christmas afternoon.

Chris gently tucked me into the passenger seat. There wasn't much traffic, so it felt like we were at the hospital in half the time it normally took to get there. The doctor had everything ready for me to get right through the ER. Within a matter of minutes, the doctors had me on IV heparin. It thinned my blood and dissolved the clots, thus saving my life that Christmas Day.

Later that week my spiritual friend Ken called to check on me. I was sharing my story about Christmas Day, and he just about dropped the phone. He said he knew something was going on because despite having a house full of people over for Christmas lunch, he felt the desperate need to pray for me intently and thus excused himself from the table to do so. We determined that the time I was so desperately praying for a miracle he was also praying for the same thing for me but had no idea why, other than that spiritual tug on his heart. As we travel along on our spiritual journey, we begin to realize those heart tugs are unquestionably God's Holy Spirit speaking to us. These are tugs we cannot ignore and should not dismiss. Often those tugs are answers to prayers that others need, like I so desperately needed that Christmas Day. Thank you, God, for your unfailing love and those tugs on our hearts!

CHAPTER 9

How Much Can We Endure?

(Age 31)

"So do not fear, for I am with you; do not be dismayed, for I am your God. I will strengthen you and help you; I will uphold you with my righteous right hand" (Isaiah 41:10).

This was one Christmas gift that was like no other! To this day I still sit and reflect on how amazing God's power really is and how blessed I was that Christmas Day. Each Christmas is a reminder that all things ARE possible with Him. I prayed, "Thank you, God, for this miracle of healing and the best Christmas gift of all – the birth of Jesus – for through Him we are made whole again."

"Honey, I feel blessed that, through a miracle, a senior radiologist came into the hospital on Christmas day last year, of all days, and picked up MY films to save my life! What a gift that was, huh?" I said smiling. "And although my condition isn't improving much, God has a plan for me, and I can't give up," I said to Chris. He always looked at me with such amazement, wondering where I found the strength to remain so positive. He was closest to me and with me more than anyone else, so he experienced everything right along with me. He took care of me with whatever I needed, like lifting my head to help me drink water when I was too weak to lift it myself or just holding me when life got overwhelming. Despite being by my side, his faith in God was not where mine was and that weighed heavily on my heart. I would frequently pray, *Jesus please hear my prayer, please heal me, so I can go out and do your work. Help me find a way to share the faith you have put in my heart with Chris, with my family, and with the world!*

It was challenging trying to function on a daily basis despite feeling like I had an ongoing case of the flu, and it was hard not to get discouraged with treatment after treatment failing, but I was thankful for every day ... even my sick days. It was quite a roller coaster ride. It seems we would start a new treatment that would work fairly well for a period of time, and then just as all our hopes would rise the treatment would fail, crushing our hopes once again.

My faith remained constant, but I was always challenged with questions from others, such as, why is God putting you through so much? How could a loving God do this? How can your faith be so strong? I would explain that once I opened my heart and mind to God, He took care of the rest. I had peace knowing I could trust Him. The only way I can think to describe it is that I felt like I was a little girl again, learning how to swim. I can envision my dad standing in the chest-high pool water in our backyard, his arms reaching towards me gently persuading me to trust him and jump. Although I was scared, I closed my eyes, and I blindly jumped into the pool knowing he would catch me ... and that in his arms I would be safe.

Despite feeling ill, I tried to balance being a wife, a mom, and an employee, but it was difficult at times. God helped me do it by giving me strength and an incredible attitude! They say what doesn't kill us makes us stronger. If that's true, then I should be the strongest person in the universe! I would remind myself that life has to go on, and I knew I could not let this disease control me; I *had* to show it who's the boss! The doctors always seemed amazed at my attitude and strength. Numerous times they saw me pull through difficulties caused by my disease, and this didn't normally happen with most patients suffering in the same manner. Some things I rebounded from were certainly not possible according to any medical book. However, they were possible in one very important book ... the Bible.

I focused daily on my faith and never gave up hope. I continued to thank God for the blessing of this disease and the lives I had been able to touch along this journey. I prayed for Him to work through me to help others with true testimonies of His healing power. I was blessed with trusting God's plan for me and with the unbelievable peace He had given me that still remained. I felt there was a plan in all this – an important one. So I would not give up and felt excited for what God was doing in my life.

My doctors tried numerous treatments, all of which failed. I researched the Internet constantly and contacted other patients around the world who were facing similar issues. I was hoping we could share some information and find the magic cure we were all so desperately seeking. Unbeknownst to me, sharing my health updates on the Internet with people around the world was serving as an inspiration to many, particularly when they were finding themselves facing a challenging day of normal stresses. I would receive emails from people sharing with me how my strength and faith inspired them to get out of bed every day, and how it made the crosses they had to bear seem so insignificant. Someone once emailed me this incredible story:

The Cross

A young woman, who was at the end of her rope
and saw no way out, dropped to her knees in prayer.
"Lord, I can't go on," she said. "I have too heavy a
cross to bear." The Lord replied, "My child, if you
can't bear its weight, just place your cross inside this
room. Then, open that other door and pick out any
cross you wish." The woman was filled with relief
and said, "Thank you, Lord," and she did as she was
told. Upon entering the other door, she saw many
crosses, some so large the tops were not visible.
Then, she spotted a tiny cross leaning against a far
wall. "I'd like that one, Lord," she whispered. And
the Lord replied, "My child, that is the cross you just
brought in."

– Author unknown

This story has served as a reminder to me throughout the years that even when the cross I have to bear seems so heavy, there is always someone out there with a bigger cross to bear; therefore, I should be thankful. I found myself at a point where I would feel more than blessed just to find a treatment that would stabilize me and give me my life back. I didn't need a cure, but I wanted to be healed so I could share with the world the true testimonies of all that is possible with God. My blood counts remained low, all of them, including platelets, red blood cells, hemoglobin, etc. I researched a treatment that looked like it might work for me. We had to keep pushing forward regardless of how small the chances were of a particular treatment helping me, and I seemed to be running out of options.

This process is called plasmapheresis; its purpose is to filter the blood in order to separate the blood cells from the antibodies by using a centrifuge. The antibodies are trapped within the filter and the filtered blood is returned to the body. The blood being returned has a reduced number of antibodies, which slows the attack on the red cells and platelets.

I would be hooked up to a machine through a two-port perma-cath that had to be surgically inserted directly into a blood vessel. One port would allow the blood to flow out into the machine and the other would return my blood to me after it had run through the centrifuge. I discussed the details with my doctors, and they agreed to try the treatment.

My appointment to have the perma-cath inserted was early in the morning with a treatment immediately following. We did the treatment and through the clear, pliable tubes the nurse thought she saw a clot in the return tube. She watched me closely afterwards but there were no signs of complications. My dad drove me home and sat with me until my husband returned home from work.

Once my husband was home, he decided to do some work in the backyard. I walked back to talk with him and noticed I could hardly breathe. I had to sit down because my pulse started racing very fast. It felt as if my heart was going to beat out of my chest. Chris yelled to my dad, "Ted, please get the phone right away. We have to call the doctor, something is really wrong with Sandi." He called my doctor and was told to take me to the ER immediately! I was trying to breathe, but it was becoming more and more difficult. This was very different from the feeling I'd had when my counts crashed to critical levels. *Should we call an ambulance?* I thought. It was very scary not being able to get air into my lungs. I prayed God would help me with the anxious feelings I was having, and that we could get to the hospital ... soon!

We arrived at the hospital, but I could not walk from the car to the ER. Chris pulled up, jumped out of the car, and grabbed a wheelchair. He picked me up and gently placed me in the wheelchair. He scurried me right to the triage area. As usual, the ER was packed but my doctor had called letting them know I would be arriving soon. He explained my complicated history and how I needed to be evaluated as soon as possible. The nurse was checking my vitals including checking the oxygen levels using a pulse oximeter. I saw the concern in her face as she was reading the display. She excused herself and quickly walked back to the ER area where the doctors were located. A doctor came out with her, and they brought me back immediately to be evaluated by a team of doctors. They helped lift me from the wheelchair and onto one of the small ER cart beds. They quickly changed me into a gown and started placing those sticky pads all over my chest to monitor my heart. My heart rate was extremely high and my blood pressure was not stable. At the same time, they were starting an IV in one arm and pulling blood from the other. I was still having a very difficult time trying to breathe. I could not get in enough oxygen no matter how hard I tried.

They rolled me down to have a lung CT scan. I felt so lost, alone, and afraid. I was helped onto the table for the lung scan. The technician shot the dye into my IV and then left the room while the machine talked to me telling me to hold my breath as it guided me into the scan for pictures. While the pictures were being evaluated, I sat there in that dark, cold CT scan room feeling a bit overwhelmed and scared. I wished my husband could put his arms around me and let me know all was going to be fine. I prayed, sharing with God how scared I was and letting Him know how alone I felt, but I also prayed, "God, I trust your plan; please be with me and give me peace and strength to face this with You by my side!" I stared at the computer screen that showed my lung images and saw what appeared to be a hologram of Jesus' face. I blinked my eyes a few times to ensure what I was seeing was really there, and the image did not change. I looked around the room for the technician, but he was not there. I continued to stare at those black and white images, but Jesus' face was very clear to me. It sent chills down my spine. I did not feel alone any longer and knew that no matter what was ahead, I had to trust God.

I was brought back to the ER where the doctor who was assigned to my case was watching the heart monitor closely. He did not like the way my heart rate was sporadic, so he yelled for the nurse to inject something into my IV STAT. STAT is a medical term used for when something urgent needs to be done immediately. Within seconds, my heart rate bottomed out, and it felt as if an elephant was sitting on my chest. I could not get any air; I could not breathe! I was scared and the fear I saw in my husband's and dad's faces was too much to handle. I tried to get the words out, "I love you. Please let Tyler know how much I love him," but not a sound came out. I squeezed my husband's hand as hard as I could, holding on for dear life as I felt warm tears rolling down my face.

I prayed to Jesus that my prayer would be heard and that He would send me another miracle. I had faith that He would answer my prayer. By this time, all of the doctors from the ER were frantically scurrying around my bed. My husband looked like he was in shock, and I saw a tear rolling down his face. After he saw my heart rate bottom out on the monitor, I could see in his face that he knew this time truly was it ... I was not going to pull out of this one. How could I? When I glanced up I saw no activity on the heart monitor – did the connections come undone? How could it show nothing, but yet I could still see all that was going on? I lay there with tears rolling down the side of my face waiting for Jesus to come – either to heal me or to call me home. I was scared at the thought of leaving my family, leaving this world, but I knew I had to trust in Him. Would I be able to hold my son again? I prayed in my heart, *I trust you God; please be with me and send me a miracle, because with you all things are possible.* Would He hear my prayer and send me another miracle?

Suddenly I felt something that is difficult to describe. It was as if God Himself reached down from heaven and placed His hand on my head. I felt a warm, tingling feeling – almost like when your arm falls asleep, but with a warm and peaceful feeling. The tingling then went slowly from my head and worked its way down to my toes. I felt as if Jesus was taking His hand and moving it over my body to heal me. The tingling continued to work its way down to my toes and then out of my body. At that very moment, the monitors went completely normal.

The doctors were frantically looking around at each other asking, "Who did something? What did you give her? What happened?" They all looked at each other puzzled because none of them had given me any medication or done anything to stabilize me. I could tell by their facial expressions and their quiet discussions that they were searching for a scientific reason that would explain what had just transpired. No matter how much they tried to explain or make sense of it scientifically, I knew exactly what had happened … Jesus DID put His healing hand on me. God answered my prayer once again because I called out to Him and believed I would receive an answer … He sent me another miracle.

We later found out that what I had was a pulmonary embolism (a blood clot that had traveled to my lung). The blood thinner had been stopped so I could have the perma-cath inserted. This resulted in my blood being too thick during the plasmapheresis treatment. For most people, a pulmonary embolism is fatal. After learning this, we understood why the doctors were so worried and then so puzzled when I spontaneously stabilized. It was then that I thanked God once again for all He had done in my life and for giving me another miracle. He is an awesome God!

> *"Therefore I tell you, whatever you ask for in prayer,*
> *believe that you have received it, and it will be yours"*
> *(Mark 11:24).*

CHAPTER 10

Give Me Strength

(Age 31)

"But I will restore you to health and heal your wounds, declares the LORD" (Jeremiah 30:17).

The perma-cath that had been put into place was left in so we could try some additional plasmapheresis treatments. Along with the perma-cath came a daily cleansing of the area and flushing of the port. This would help prevent any kind of infection from setting in since this port was an opening right to my bloodstream. We were hopeful that this treatment would be the answer since so many other things had failed. We had found out not long ago that I was pregnant again (this was the 4th pregnancy). We were not trying to become pregnant, but it appeared God had different plans. Tyler prayed for a baby brother or sister every day. When we made it past 8 weeks, we shared the ultrasound picture with him and explained how strong the baby's heartbeat was. He was so excited that he took the ultrasound picture to school with him to show his teacher.

Later that week within an hour of flushing my port, I spiked a fever of 104. Chris had to rush me to the ER. This time was even more worrisome because we knew we had a pregnancy to think about as well. I became quite ill – weak, nauseated, jaundiced. The doctors admitted me to the hospital so they could determine why I was so ill. They decided to remove the perma-cath and found that it had bacteria on the tip; thus, when I had flushed it earlier that day, I had pushed the infection into my bloodstream. I became septic so was transferred to the ICU. Being septic is a toxic condition resulting from the spread of bacteria in the bloodstream.

My blood disease was very active at this time and was killing off my red blood cells and platelets faster than they were being produced. The doctors were monitoring my blood counts frequently. They all became very concerned when my bone marrow shut down. They suspected a possible Parvo-B virus but were not certain. Because my bone marrow shut down, it was therefore not producing cells to replace the ones that my body was killing off. The infection was still rampant in my body. Many patients do not survive a septic infection of this kind, let alone complicating the situation with the critical state my blood disorder was in at the time.

The OB/GYN team came in to see us. They explained the seriousness of my health situation. They said that they had to treat me before the baby. I felt as if they were asking me for permission to abort my baby. I looked at them and said, "If this baby is not meant to survive then God will make that decision. We will not." I think they were shocked at my response. However, as much as I knew how serious my condition was, I could not make the decision to give up the life of the baby growing inside of me, even if it meant saving my own life.

Multiple antibiotics and steroids were going into my IV. My blood counts were critically low, so they were giving me 6 units of blood at the same time. I was praying my body would not kill the cells as fast as they were giving them to me because this was my only hope. The doctors told my family how serious my condition was. I lay in my hospital bed staring death in the face, again, not knowing what the next few hours would bring. I found myself praying again, even harder than before, knowing I was fighting for my life as well as the one growing inside of me. "Jesus, please hear my prayer and give me the strength to endure all I am facing. I believe in You and know that through You I will be healed." My prayer was always very specific. I knew somehow I had to endure this so that I could share my story with others. My fervent heart's desire has always been to help people find their way to Christ. I want to help them understand that when we believe with COMPLETE faith, all things are possible with God – including being healed.

By the next morning, my blood counts began stabilizing, and my bone marrow started working again; thankfully, the infection was coming under control, and we were very grateful for yet another miracle from God. I felt so happy and then the thought crossed my mind, *is the baby okay?* My happiness soon turned to worry.

They brought an ultrasound machine into ICU. The technician set up the machine and squirted warm, gooey liquid onto the ultrasound wand. Just as she was starting to place the wand onto my belly, I became overwhelmed with a feeling of sadness. Somehow at that moment, I knew the baby did not make it. I watched the ultrasound monitor and my eyes filled with tears. There on the screen was our baby. But, it was no longer an image of a healthy baby with a flickering heartbeat – instead, our baby was lifeless. The heart, although still visible, no longer flickered. My tears would not stop. We had lost the baby. My heart was heavy, but I knew we had to trust God's plan despite the pain I felt in my heart. It was a very difficult time, especially a few days later when I was brought down to have the D & C surgery necessary to remove the baby.

We knew it would be hard to explain the miscarriage to Tyler, but we focused on the blessing of God pulling me out of another "impossible" situation. We were very thankful that I was still alive. As hard as it was telling Tyler, I was blessed with the opportunity of life and being able to be there to comfort him. I still felt in my heart that our family was not quite complete yet but trusted God's plan. After all we had been through, I knew we could not handle this on our own. We had to give it to God … completely. In His time, if we were meant to have another baby in our family, we would be blessed with one.

CHAPTER 11

Angels

(Age 32)

"For God does speak – now one way, now another – though man
may not perceive it. In a dream, in a vision of the night, when
deep sleep falls on men as they slumber in their beds, he may
speak in their ears ..." (Job 33:14-16)

"I have to tell you about a dream I had. It was amazing," I
said to my dad. When I had just woken up from sleep and the
dream was fresh in my mind, I thought to myself, *I can't help*
but wonder if it is God's way of letting me know not to give up
because He knows I am growing weak physically with all that
I have been facing. I didn't know how much longer I could
go on, and I knew I would need Jesus to carry me yet again.
My faith had not faltered. I remained strong in my faith, but
I was coming to a point where I was letting my family know
that if God's plan was to call me home, then I was ready to go,
because physically I was not sure I could go on much longer.

"I'd love to hear about your dream, honey," my dad said as he pulled his chair up closer to my bed.

"I dreamed that I was in bed and very ill. A woman walked into my room. She looked like an angel, Dad. Just her presence surrounded me with comfort and peace. She was a petite, beautiful woman with dark hair and dark eyes. She spoke to me in English, but she had a thick accent, and I couldn't tell where she was originally from. She walked over to my bed, and it was as if she was doing a healing of the hands. I woke up feeling hope that I am going to be healed. It was the most hope I have felt in a long time."

My dad just smiled and said, "Well, you know this wouldn't be the first time that God has sent you visions in a dream, so I think that is great, kiddo!" I smiled and was thankful for the strength and hope the dream had given to me. Was God sending me an angel? Mark 16 tells us that believers will be able to use their hands to heal the sick.

> *"… they will place their hands on sick people, and they will get well" (Mark 16:18).*

Many months had passed, and I was still very ill. My blood counts would not stabilize. I was going into the hospital weekly for blood transfusions because my body continued to kill my blood cells. I was on so many steroids that the side effects were overwhelming. I was failing all treatments. I had just heard about a new treatment (Antibiotic Therapy Treatment) that was helping some Lupus patients. Although I did not have Lupus, I had many of the same symptoms, and since nothing else was working, what did I have to lose? I tried to convince my doctor, but he seemed reluctant and unsure of it. I thought I would gather more research and keep pushing forward for this treatment.

I ached all of the time, so much that my sister-in-law Carrie would give me weekly massages. She was a massage therapist in addition to her daily job at a marketing agency. It's amazing how God puts people in our lives just when we need them the most. She had moved in with us trying to save some money but ended up being there to help with Ty and anything else we needed as we made numerous trips to the hospital. My dad also felt a strong urge to walk away from a good paying job and retire early. He did not know why, but he listened to the tug on his heart. Neither one of us had any idea that he would be the one God chose to help take me to the hospital for all of the blood transfusions and treatments I would need over the next couple of years. I believe with all my heart that there are many earth angels, and I had been blessed with a few.

Carrie set up the massage table to give me a massage because I was especially hurting that day. During the massages we would talk about God and how He was giving me the strength to face all of this. At the time, she was struggling with her faith. She believed in a higher power but wasn't sure about the whole God or Jesus idea. I did not know at the time that all of the things she went through with us would be the foundation she needed to build a strong faith in God, which she has today. She is an incredible soul. She is often there to remind me of

God's promise and undying love when I have a weak moment in my faith. It is amazing the lives that are touched and guided to God when we hold strong to our faith, especially when facing such adversity.

Shortly after my massage, I began feeling pain that started in my neck and worked its way down to my arms, spine, and then legs. I woke up my husband and told him we needed to go to the closest emergency room. I knew I couldn't make it to the University of Chicago. He drove me to the local ER, and by the time we arrived there, I was crying from all of the pain. It felt as if someone was ripping the muscles right off of my bones. It was the most excruciating pain I had ever experienced. I could not move any of my limbs because the pain was too intense. Chris lifted me out of the car and put me into a wheelchair.

I was placed on a bed in the back of the ER and left there. It seemed like forever before a doctor saw me. They would not give me any pain medicine, and it became obvious that they thought I was some druggie just wanting a pain med fix. After what seemed like an eternity, I started screaming to get my husband in there NOW!!! It took fifteen minutes of me screaming before they finally got him. I asked him to page my doctors at U of C right away and get them on the phone. He did so and then handed the phone to the doctor. I have never seen doctors move so fast or be so apologetic. They immediately started an IV and gave me strong pain medicine. They were prepping me to be transferred by ambulance to U of C.

Even the strongest pain medicine would not take the pain away. The pain of being loaded in the ambulance, the pain of being jostled in the ambulance, which felt like we were hitting every bump in the road, and then the pain of being unloaded from the ambulance was unbearable. I had no idea what was going on because I had never felt anything like this before. I was admitted to the hospital and multiple tests were performed. One of the tests showed transverse myelitis, but the pain in all of my limbs did not quite fit a particular diagnosis. Transverse myelitis is a disease of the spinal cord that generally causes weakness in the legs. I had been followed by the hematology team due to my blood disorder but was told they were going to be calling in a rheumatology team as well. The doctors were unsure of my outcome because it was not clear what was causing the pain and weakness I was experiencing.

My dad was by my side as usual. I am blessed with a great dad. As I lay resting in my hospital bed he was flipping through the TV channels when suddenly there was a knock at the door and in walked an African American gentleman in his thirties wearing a green robe like a priest would wear. He resembled my closest spiritual friend Ken thus giving me an instant feeling of comfort as he entered my room. He wore a brown, wooden cross around his neck that very much brought Jesus to my mind. He walked over to my bed. He said, "Hi Sandi, I'm Father John. Would it be okay if I prayed with you?" I was surprised he had called me Sandi, because everyone but my friends and family called me Sandra because that was my full name shown in my medical chart. I sensed there was something different about him, but I wasn't sure what it was.

I was thankful someone came into my room to pray with me … *for* me. I had little hope left and felt myself succumbing to what seemed to be God's plan. My fight appeared rapidly to be coming to an end. My options for treatment had quickly dwindled over the last few months. I needed another miracle. I was very ill and now found myself in a hospital bed with limited movement of my arms and legs.

He took my hand, bowed his head, and began to pray. He prayed, "Jesus, please heal Sandi. You have heard her prayers and her cries for healing for sometime now so that she can go out and do Your work … to go and share the wonderful blessings You have done in her life, the true testimonies to You, Lord. Heal this girl and let her begin the work You have planned for her." He continued on with his prayers, and the more he prayed the more I was in awe at what God was doing. I opened my eyes and stared at him, not believing what I was hearing. He was praying the same very personal, private prayers, that only *I* had prayed to God. No one else would have known those prayers, yet there he stood in my room asking Jesus for the same things my very soul was seeking. He finished with "Amen" and left telling me that he hoped God would heal me soon so I could begin helping others.

When he left, I looked to my dad and said, "I don't even know what to say right now." I explained how Father John had just prayed my very personal prayers that only God would have known. My dad just shook his head in awe saying, "Sandi, there is no doubt you are one of God's special children. I don't know what to say either." My mom has always told me the same thing. I think both of my parents had witnessed the true power of God so many times through my journey that they felt there was a special plan for me. I believe we are all God's special children. However, we have to first open our hearts and minds to Him, and then He will pour out His blessings on anyone who believes in Him.

Later when the nurses came in we mentioned Father John's visit and how much it meant to me. They all looked at us puzzled saying they did not know of a Father John and had not seen anyone come into or leave my room. My dad and I looked at each other with amazement and got chills down our spines. Was Father John real or was he an angel?

~~~~~~~~~~

I had progressively worsened throughout the night. I could feel my legs but I couldn't move them. I felt incredibly weak as if complete atrophy set in. The next day my dad came back to visit me, and we heard doctors talking outside of my room. We could hear the rustling of the papers in my chart and their discussion of my rare case. The door opened and in walked a woman doctor who looked familiar. Just the sight of her brought me comfort and hope. She had the presence of an angel. My eyes filled with tears, and I turned to my dad and said, "Dad, that's her, that IS her!! That is the woman in my dream, the one that healed me." My dad's jaw dropped, and he said, "She is just like you described her from your dream." We both just stared at her in awe.

She approached my bed as I stared at her with tears streaming down my face. I had to tell her about my dream. I said, "I am very sorry if this seems odd, but I am overcome with hope right now. I dreamt about you. God sent you to heal me. I have been sick for so long and am failing every treatment. Just when I thought I was at my end with all of this pain – God sent me an angel in my dream, and you are that angel." She just smiled, and we shared an instant spiritual bond. She is different from any other doctor I had ever met. She seems to bring the combination of medicine and spirituality to her treatment just by her presence. She introduced herself as Dr. Nadera Sweiss. I asked where she was from, and when she replied "Jordan," I couldn't believe it! She was from the Holy Land – of all the places in the world.

We discussed my case in detail. I shared with her the details of the Antibiotic Therapy that I was so desperate to try. She researched it and agreed it was worth a shot. She also wanted to try a new drug (Cell Cept) they were using on transplant patients. Although there were no medical findings to support it being used in anyone with my condition, she felt guided to try it in my case. She did not ignore that tug on her heart, the one we need to learn to trust and listen to despite our hesitations, despite our occupation, sometimes in defiance of any human logic.

Prior to Dr. Sweiss walking into my room, I had hit rock-bottom. There were no known medical treatments remaining for me to try. There appeared to be little hope but I trusted God's plan and remembered the dream He had sent me ... a dream of hope. After all when we hit rock-bottom there is nowhere to go but up, right? I knew to hold strong to my faith and not give up. She started a regimen of the Cell Cept and Minocin (the Antibiotic Therapy). Within a couple of months my blood counts had stabilized for the FIRST time in years and I had regained complete control of my arms and legs. I was in awe, once again, at all that is possible with God. He sent me another miracle! My faith was strengthened so much knowing God stayed true to His promise ... He did not forsake me.

CHAPTER 12

Perseverance ... Finding Inner Strength

(Age 32)

"... strengthening the disciples and encouraging them to remain true to the faith. 'We must go through many hardships to enter the kingdom of God'" (Acts 14:22).

The treatments Dr. Sweiss introduced put my blood disease into remission. It was great to feel good again! I knew I had felt sick, but honestly I had no idea how bad it really was until I felt well again. Every time I have the flu it reminds me of how horrible I felt on a daily basis for years ... not days, but years! It was amazing how God was giving me my life back.

Day by day, we were able to get back to some normalcy in our lives. That included the craziness life sends each of us whether it is running our children around for different sports activities, completing a major project at work, helping care for a parent, or being there for a friend in need. Life happens, doesn't it? It felt good to be part of life again; a life where I could take more than a few steps before I had to sit down and catch my breath. Soon Chris, Tyler, and I would once again do things that normal families could do, things most families either take for granted or don't take time to do because they are caught up in the busyness of "life."

We were able to take long walks along a wooded path in late fall when the air was cold enough to bundle up but not so cold that we needed hats and gloves. It was nice to breathe that wonderful, brisk fall air and take in the beauty of God's handiwork. We were surrounded by multiple colors of bright yellow, vibrant orange, and fiery red leaves displayed on the trees hugging the path on which we walked. It felt like heaven to me! I definitely had learned to appreciate the little things in life.

The condition of my blood disease was fantastic! Every blood count continued to show normal results. I stared at the first few test results because I felt like I was dreaming – it seemed too good to be true. Even so, it WAS true, my blood counts were normal – every part of them! I had the energy and health to be a wife, a mother, a daughter, a sister, and a friend again. I could be me! Being a type "A" personality, trust me – that was saying a lot! I could do the big things as well as the little things that we all too often take for granted. I thanked God every day for giving my life back to me.

If only those who have good health would realize what a special gift God has given them. They have the freedom to go after their dreams. It is easy to take life for granted, especially living in a country where anything is possible. Seeing "In God

We Trust" inscribed on the back of a U.S. dollar bill suddenly brought new meaning to me. The United States represents freedom just as trusting in God brings freedom. If we trust in God, we can have freedom with endless possibilities. This freedom represents the peace and happiness He wants for each of us.

We all have the vision to see the good in our lives that God surrounds us with all of the time, but we have to have our eyes *open* in order to see it. Only we are in control of whether we are going to be happy today or not. It is easy to blame others for our unhappiness, but if we focus on the blessings in our lives, then we are one step closer to God. Our focus then becomes the good that's in our lives; we no longer focus on the negativity, which can easily rob us of the happiness God wants for each of us.

~~~~~~~~~~

My blood counts remained stable, but I noticed a strange pain in my right hip. It was almost as if my lower back or tailbone was somehow out of alignment, which sent shooting pains into my hip. I made an appointment with the doctor because I knew I needed to have it evaluated. It seemed the pain was progressing pretty quickly. The initial doctor dismissed it as nothing, but my intuition was telling me it was something. I kept pushing for testing and treatment until my regular doctor recommended I see an orthopedic surgeon for a consultation.

Throughout the years I had learned to listen to that tug on my heart because for me, it was definitely God speaking to me, whether directly or through an angel speaking on His behalf. It is incredible what happens when we start paying attention to exactly how often we are being guided to do something. The signs are there – we should not ignore them and what God is trying to tell us. If we regularly ignored stop signs and stoplights in traffic, barely missing getting hit, how many times would we be lucky enough to cruise through unharmed? More often than not, harm would befall us, which we could've spared ourselves had we paid attention to the stop sign in front of us. Likewise, please make the decision to be safe with God and stop when His spirit tugs at your heart to not move forward, but definitely press on when you sense He is telling you to go!

~~~~~~~~~~

I was able to get an appointment with one of the top orthopedic surgeons at the University of Chicago. What a blessing that was! It was awesome how God seemed to perfectly line up just the right people to help me along my journey. The doctor evaluated me, ran some tests, and then reviewed the results with Chris and me. We were surprised at the diagnosis. He said I had a condition called AVN (Avascular Necrosis). "What?" I said as I looked at him baffled, trying to understand a medical term that once again sounded like another language to me. He explained that it is a condition where the bone tissue dies due to lack of blood supply. They believed the prednisone could be the main contributor. All I knew was that it was already some months ago when I'd had that episode of excruciating pain in my bones and so finding a treatment as soon as possible was critical.

He explained, "Well, I have good news and bad news. The good news is that although the left hip shows the AVN too, we have a 50% chance of saving that hip by doing a hip core decompression surgery." I sat there staring at him trying to comprehend what he was saying. My mind wandered, thinking, *My left hip? What do you mean my left hip? Only my right hip had the pain.* He continued, "The bad news is that your right hip has advanced AVN so you will most likely need a total hip replacement. You are young, and we do not like to perform total hip replacements unless we absolutely have to do them." *Did he just say total hip replacement? What does core decompression mean? I am only thirty-two years old!* Many things were flashing through my head. I was very active and loved to work out, run, ski, and skate, plus, it was only a few months ago that I had just gotten my life back! The thought of a total hip replacement seemed discouraging, but I reminded myself that I could get through this … I knew I could. I said to myself with resolve, *God will give me the strength! Look at all I have already faced. He will get me through this storm too.*

He said, "Since things seem to be progressing pretty quickly, we need to schedule the core decompression as soon as possible. It will be a difficult surgery recovery because you will not be able to put weight on the leg for six weeks." He explained, "The core decompression is a technique where we drill into the bone to remove a portion of it, which allows increased blood flow by stimulating growth of new blood vessels."

Just the thought of such a procedure made me blurt out, "Ouch!" as I cringed in imaginary pain. Chris reached over and grabbed my hand to ensure I knew he would be there to help me, and to once again carry the weight of things that seemed difficult to bear, just as St. Christopher was said to have done for Jesus. Next to God, Chris was my hero! We met with the nurses and scheduled the pre-operative appointment as well as the surgery.

I will not deny that Satan tried to put worry and doubt in my heart. I was determined to focus on my blessings. My blood counts were still normal – that was huge! I cannot imagine what would have happened if I had still been in a critical state when I developed AVN. How could I have dealt with being so sick on top of the horrible pain this condition brought? I was quickly learning that God truly does only give us what we can handle. I was determined to face this new set of challenges with optimism, just as I had faced all of the others. I pushed the worry out and replaced it with more trust in God. My heart felt good because I knew God would not forsake me. Medically there was only a fifty percent chance of saving my left hip, but I had God on my side, so even if there was only a one percent chance, nothing, and I mean NOTHING, was impossible with Him. I felt strongly there was a plan, and I knew to be patient and trust Him.

The core decompression surgery went great! I was sent home on crutches with strict instructions not to put any weight on the leg. We lived in a beautiful two-story home that had many stairs leading up to the level where the bedrooms were located. This was the kind of lovely home I had only dreamt of having some day as a young girl. It's amazing the blessings that are brought into your life once you open your heart to God.

When I hobbled through the front door on my crutches, the stairs were the first thing I saw. I thought, *Wow, it is going to be awesome that soon I will be flying up and down those stairs again – woo hoo!* I settled in on the couch for the day and figured I would camp out downstairs for a few days until my hip was doing a little better. Tyler ran over to hug me and welcome me home. I had really missed him! He was now six years old and being quite a trooper with all he had to go through with his mommy.

The next six weeks were not easy doing everything on crutches, but I managed. My shoulders really started to hurt. The doctors contributed the pain to the length of time I had spent on the crutches. My right hip hurt more and more. It was bearing my entire weight, which aggravated the condition even more. By the time the six weeks had passed, my right hip was in unbelievable pain and my shoulders were a close second.

I went in for my six-week evaluation, and we were pleased to hear that the core decompression was a success. The fifty percent chance ended up being a hundred percent with God on my side. We were able to save the hip! I couldn't believe how many blessings came mixed in with all of the challenges. No matter what challenge was staring me in the face, I found myself becoming excited, just waiting to see what God was going to do next. The stronger my belief, the more God delivered His promise. I was amazed over and over again at all that was possible. To think it had been there the whole time, and all I had to do was accept Him. And, yes, at first that meant blindly leaping, but it was worth the jump! It was definitely worth the jump!

Over the next few weeks my right hip continued to deteriorate to such a degree that at the follow-up appointment the X-ray showed that the hip had collapsed. The bone was jagged, which explained why I would scream in pain whenever I tried to stand up. It was tearing into the surrounding muscles. Despite being on pain pills, the pain was so intense that when I tried to move around, such as to get into bed or go to the restroom, it seemed nearly impossible to do. Tears would roll down my face because it hurt so much – just constant, searing pain. Even lying down without moving a muscle was extremely painful. I could no longer dress myself or do simple things I had once taken for granted, like shaving my legs. I was determined to get through this latest ordeal, so I continued to try to do things for myself, but each time the jagged bone would send sharp, stabbing pain through my hip like I'd been stabbed. Soon I found myself in a wheelchair and no longer able to walk.

My shoulders continued to worsen and soon started hurting as much as my hip. The doctors evaluated the pain and determined it wasn't from the crutches but instead was also from the AVN, which had now advanced rapidly and taken hold in my shoulders. I was only in my thirties and my bones were deteriorating more every day. I was facing bilateral shoulder arthroplasty surgery; a surgery that replaced the ball part of the shoulder with a metal shaft. I sat in shock when the doctor told me all my joints were dying at once. I had to make a decision as to whether I should have my shoulder surgeries done first or my right-hip replacement. I was a young mom; how was I going to take care of my family?

My shoulders were bad. I could barely move them and could no longer dress myself, but more sadly, it was impossible for me to hug Tyler or my husband. It was as if there was an invisible spacer between my elbows that would not allow my arms to reach together. It was difficult to raise a glass in order to get a drink, and I felt bad not being able to help with Tyler or anything else that needed to be done around our house. I had become helpless, and I so desperately wanted to hug my baby!

It was difficult having my normal life back for a few precious months only to have it taken away again, but I remained strong in my faith, and I knew I could do this. Despite my discouragement, it was amazing how once my faith was in the right place, my entire perspective changed. Many years ago Ken tried telling me that, but I wasn't always listening. Had I understood the peace and strength it would bring, I would have opened my mind and heart sooner instead of feeling sorry for myself when something bad would happen to me.

I could only think this is what David must have felt like when he faced Goliath. David's faith was unshakable, especially after God had delivered him from the lion and the bear. *"The Lord who delivered me from the paw of the lion and the paw of the bear will deliver me from the hand of this Philistine" (1 Samuel 17:37).* David was a young boy, yet he stood up against this strong giant saying *"... You come against me with sword and spear and javelin, but I come against you in the name of the Lord .... This day the Lord will hand you over to me, and ... the whole world will know that there is a God in Israel" (1 Samuel 17:45-46).* I knew that if he could defeat a giant with a stone to prove there was a God, I could also withstand all I was facing. I prayed that my triumphs could be testimonies proving that there is a God – a God who still does miracles, even today.

Each day was a challenge, but with God, I was ready to fight whatever battle I needed to fight. The simplest tasks seemed monumental at times. I could have easily become discouraged knowing I couldn't get myself a drink of water, bathe myself, brush my teeth, dress myself, play with my son, or take care of my family – but who was on my side? Yes, God was! The pain was a true test of my faith, but if remaining strong in my faith while enduring all of this pain and suffering would help even one person open their mind and heart to Jesus, it would be worth it. The same peace and strength are out there for each of us, so I knew I had to stay strong!

Although once a very independent woman, I was learning to surrender because I could not do it on my own any longer. I continued to turn to God for strength. I knew that, despite how difficult things were at the time, He would be with me through each surgery and that some day I would be free of pain once again. We go through things for a reason. There always is a silver lining to the gray clouds, but we have to look for it and never give up hope. I felt strongly about this one, and although I did not understand the reason for all of these surgeries at the time, a year later it would become very clear to me.

~~~~~~~~~~

Finally, it was time to have my hip replacement. The doctors made it clear it was going to be a hard recovery with daily physical therapy needed. My mom came to stay with us for a month. She knew it would not be possible for Chris to take that much time off from work, and helping me bathe wouldn't exactly be something my dad would do. What an angel she is! I was so thankful she was unselfishly offering to help us for an entire month. I really have been blessed with two incredible parents, and actually, an incredible family.

I said to my family, "Guys, don't be so worried. It is awesome that my blood counts are stable for the surgery, and God is right here with me. Trust in His plan and know it will all work out." They each leaned down to hug and kiss me before I was wheeled off to the operating room for my right hip replacement. I knew the risks I was facing. I had an extremely complicated history with a medical chart a few inches thick to prove it. The doctors had to stop my blood thinner for each surgery, which was extremely risky. When I am not on blood thinner, I run the risk of throwing a blood clot; a clot that could result in taking a wife and mother away from a young family. In addition, any trauma could trigger my disease to go into a hyper-state causing another attack on my cells. This would lower my blood counts, thus adding more risk. There also was increased risk of a post-operative infection due to a suppressed immune system from the medications I was on. We would then have to re-introduce the blood thinner with the risk of bleeding out if things were not healing inside as expected. Despite all of these risks, I had so much hope and peace even in this scary situation. Soon we were in the ice-cold operating room and the nurses were moving me from the cart to the operating table. Within minutes they had me hooked up to different IVs. They placed a mask over my nose and mouth and asked me to count backwards from 100. I started counting "100, 99, 98, 97, 96..." and I drifted off to sleep.

My husband was very nervous in the waiting room, as was the rest of my family. My brother, who does not like hospitals at all, was there too. He knew how serious this surgery was going to be for me. They all knew what could easily happen in that operating room. My husband, mom, dad, and brother found a table off to the far left side of the surgery waiting area to get settled in for what could be many hours. Despite my assurances to them that all was going to be okay, they were worried. Before my surgery I had prayed that somehow I would be able to figure out a way to take the faith and peace from my heart and put it into theirs. I found myself praying often for those around me, asking God to open their minds so they could have the same incredible peace and strength He had blessed me with.

Heather, my earth angel nurse, knew I was having surgery, so she came down to check on them. She was so sweet and kind, quite an incredible girl. She knew exactly what we needed to get through all of this scary medical stuff. She was single and had recently broken up with her boyfriend. A couple of weeks prior to my surgery, I had mentioned to her that my brother was also single, and maybe she should consider going out on a blind date with him. She said, "You have a brother?" Since Mike did not like hospitals, he had never come to visit. She did not like the idea of blind dates, so I wasn't sure how they would meet but knew if they were meant to meet, they would. Later, I was surprised to hear my brother was going to be there for the surgery and I thought maybe, just maybe, they could meet that way. It wasn't the most ideal setting, but at least they could meet each other without the awkwardness of a blind date.

Chris stood up when Heather walked in. She saw Mike and thought he was really cute, so she immediately felt nervous. I heard later that she was acting like a giddy school girl and even hid behind Chris! My brother just smiled and knew he *had* to see her again. Heather sat with my family awhile to ensure they were okay and kept checking with the nurses to see how I was doing. She wanted to ensure I was going to be okay, because the surgery was running longer than normal. She helped my family so much that day. I was thankful God worked through her to bring them the support they needed while they sat worried and scared in that hospital waiting room.

~~~~~~~~~

I made great progress the first couple of weeks after my hip replacement surgery. I was excited to go back to the surgeon for my follow-up visit so I could share all I had accomplished in physical therapy. I had just gotten past the point of feeling constant pain and saw the light at the end of the tunnel! During my follow-up appointment I was surprised to hear from the doctor that I had developed a hematoma in my right hip, and I would have to go back in for surgery to have it removed. A hematoma is when your blood collects in a certain area and is usually clotted. I had noticed a rather large lump on my right hip, but since the hip felt good, and therapy was going great, I thought it was normal swelling from the surgery. My mom had mentioned she didn't think it looked quite right. There was that mother's intuition again … a heart tug! A couple of weeks ago the thought of going right back in for surgery would've been overwhelming. It compares to what a woman might feel after just giving birth to a baby and then finding out two weeks later she would have to deliver another one. It would not be on the top of her "things to do" list! However, sitting in that doctor's office, I felt strong yet again; I knew I could do this with God on my side. Something good was going to come of all of this… something really good.

The hematoma removal went well, and I was back to therapy in no time at all. Soon I was walking with a walker, and then a cane. Yes, it was unnatural being in my early thirties walking around the neighborhood with a walker, but that was nothing. I was thankful that God had brought me through a major surgery safely, and that I could walk again. I was no longer in a wheelchair, and that was a huge gift! Despite the odds, I had made it through yet another surgery safely and with great results.

One Christmas afternoon, not long after my surgeries, I found myself scurrying around running late for a Christmas gathering. *Darn it! I forgot to wrap a gift!* I thought. I walked upstairs to our walk-in attic to get the Christmas paper and gift tags. I picked up the Christmas tags and didn't realize the package was open. Next thing I knew, 200 Christmas tags were scattered all over the floor. It was worse than a 52-card pick-up! It was 200 small Christmas tags, come on! I got down on my knees to pick up the tags, feeling very frustrated. I had no time for this! What tough luck it was dropping all of these tags! It then hit me ... I got a tear in my eye and thanked God for the ability of being able to bend down to pick up the tags that busy afternoon – because just one year ago I wasn't even able to walk! Something that would normally be a nuisance in a busy Christmas season was a special gift to me. It served as a reminder of all that we tend to take for granted and all we should be thankful for. "Thank you, God, for this mess of 200 tags in front of me and the ability to bend down to pick them up!" I started singing the words, "I'm dreaming of a White Christmas" in my head as I gathered up the Christmas tags, smiling with a thankful heart!

~~~~~~~~~~~

My two shoulder surgeries were next. Each surgery was a few months after the one prior. It was a difficult year of pain, surgery, recovery, and physical therapy but all very important to my spiritual journey. I went through five surgeries that year. Through it all I had hope, I had peace, I was happy ... I had figured out that secret, the contagious joy I had wanted so desperately when I had met Ken all those years ago. These challenges strengthened my faith and taught me very important lessons. They served as reminders not to take the small things for granted and to look for the good in all things, even the difficulties. These were not times to turn away from God but instead were times to turn towards Him. We need to learn to appreciate all that is in our lives. I learned that I had definitely taken a lot for granted in my life – like being able to walk!

It is amazing how I was able to persevere through it all – the pain, the discouragement of not being able to hug those I love so much, and knowing I had to give up my pride by becoming completely dependent on someone else. I felt blessed by having this disease, not sorry for myself – my eyes were opened to all God was doing to teach me, and it was a powerful revelation! It had taught me to persevere, and most importantly, it taught me that I could face anything with God on my side. He continued to prove to me over and over again the things that were possible with Him. The peace in your soul that comes from believing in Him so strongly does not compare to anything else on this earth!

CHAPTER 13

Bringing Two People Together

(Age 32)

"The Lord God said, 'It is not good for the man to be alone; I will make a helper suitable for him'" (Genesis 2:18).

Let's go back a bit so I can share what happened with Mike and my nurse angel Heather. Well, in my brother's words, his meddling sister decided she needed to play matchmaker one more time for her brother because her previous attempts had been so successful – actually, make that unsuccessful, but I didn't give up easily! Mike is nicknamed Pickle. When Ty was little, he couldn't say Uncle Michael so instead it came out as Uncle Mickle. One time it slipped as Uncle Pickle and we all started laughing. My family is awesome! Every time we get together we are in stitches laughing hysterically, especially at Mike. He is the baby of the family and is one of the funniest people I know! Mike's little three-year-old nephew unknowingly gave him the nickname that would stick forever – Pickle!

Back to the story ... being the matchmaker I loved to be, I told Mike about this wonderful nurse at U of C who had suddenly become single. He said to me, "Suddenly? What – did she off her ex or something?" I was cracking up laughing already. I told him that he might be able to meet her at my upcoming hip surgery.

With Mike's love for hospitals, he was all excited to get to meet a girl there. Not exactly! So as I went into surgery, Mike waited in the waiting room with our entire family present, I might add, for when he would meet Heather. I asked Mike to share his story, so in his own words, documented by Pickle, here goes:

> In walks this stunning woman. She says hi to Chris and immediately asks him for a hug. *Wonder if my sister knows about that?* She then did not let him sit down and continued to use him as a shield. I did not get a good look at her, but I could tell Chris had received a perfect haircut. I managed a smile and a hello to Heather and even stood to shake her hand. What a Casanova move, a handshake. After she left, I was grilled by my family asking me, "Why didn't you talk to her?" Like meeting a girl for the first time is something you want to do with your whole family there.
>
> Time passed and Sandi informed me that Heather was coming to her house, and that I should come down after work. Again, my sister Susan is there with her family so it is another instance of Heather meeting me in front of my whole family again. Not my style! I rush home after work so I can go to Sandi's. To my disappointment I got there thirty minutes after

Heather left. Sandi got on the phone and convinced Heather to come back. She finally agreed and showed up later in the evening.

We sat around the table and talked, although I did not say more than two words to Heather that night. The highlight was when I had to excuse myself to go use the bathroom. Little did I know the toilet upstairs did not always flush properly, and Tyler (who was about 7 or 8 at the time) had no problem announcing to the entire house that "there was poopy left in the toilet." Just as my embarrassment was at its highest point, Susan came to the rescue and took the blame. Whew – couldn't let Heather think I actually have a normal functioning bowel.

Chris started a bonfire outside, so we all gathered around the fire to talk. I think I sat next to Heather, but I still did not talk to her. When the evening came to an end she left before I could work up the courage to walk her to her car. After she left, I was again put on the spot by my sisters as to why I did not talk to her, walk her to her car, or even get her number. I asked Sandi to ask Heather if it was okay for her to give me her number. I could contact her on my own time with less of an audience.

I called Heather during the week, and we made plans to go out. Something came up, and we had to delay our first date. I suspect this was due to her other boyfriend, but I cannot get her to confirm this even after six years. The day finally arrived for our first date. I picked her up, and we went to dinner. She was wearing a nice sundress, which I now know is not normal for her, so she was out to impress, and she did impress! We finished dinner and headed to a local watering hole to meet up with some old co-workers of mine. Before going to the bar we had to stop at her place so she could change. She did not want to wear a dress to the bar, go figure. I remained a gentleman and waited for her downstairs as she went up to change. We headed out and had a few drinks. After we left the bar we returned to her house and sat on her couch and talked. We talked until 1:00 am, at which time I asked her if I could kiss her. She agreed and there were fireworks. I knew then that there was something about Heather.

I was on Cloud 9 as I drove back to Naperville in the wee hours of the morning. I was met at the door by Jinx, my cat. I proceeded to tell him all about this wonderful woman. Hey, I was a single guy living alone; who else was I supposed to tell? The next day I called Heather, and we talked for a couple of hours. We made plans to get together, and as I understand it now she viewed these as tentative plans, but that was not my impression. The next day I was still in a daze. I had finally met a good woman, and not from the Internet. I was genuinely excited to see where it would lead. I returned home from work at lunch and checked my email. There in my inbox was my Dear John letter from Heather. Apparently, she had been seeing someone else and since "He was there first" she "wanted to see where it would go." I was polite and wished her good luck but inside, I was devastated. I again confided in Jinx and asked him how someone I only went on one date with could have this effect on me? To which he responded by licking his butt.

About a month or so passed and I still had not heard from Heather, I figured she had resumed her life, and

I was just a flash in the pan. Then I received the now famous run-on email from her. Here she is emailing a guy in IT (Information Technology) from a computer with a broken spacebar. You would think she would have at least used capitalization to help with the readability, but she didn't. Here is a sample of what she sent.

HiMike,notsureifyouareinterestedornotbutIamagain singleandifyouarefreeIwouldliketogooutagain,ifyou areinterestedbutIunderstandifyouarenot.Heather"

Of course I had a stalker girl of my own I was trying to shake so I jumped at the chance. We planned a date for that weekend, but this time it was going to be on my turf. We went to a pool hall in Naperville and then to dinner. After dinner we decided to go bowling. I knew I was in for it when she pulled out her own bowling ball and shoes. We bowled and then returned to my apartment. We continued to talk (and kiss) until about 2:00 a.m. She told me she was going home, and I informed her I was concerned about her being so tired and driving so late, and so I said she could stay at my place and I would sleep on the couch.

She must have been taken aback by my question because when I asked why she said "no," all she could respond with was that she did not have a toothbrush. How many women are concerned with oral hygiene at that moment? Having been raised watching *MacGyver* as a kid I immediately went into problem-solving mode. I said I would go across the street to Jewel and buy her one. Stunned, she agreed, so off I went at 2:00 am to Jewel to buy a toothbrush. Never even thinking I just left a stranger in my apartment. I returned from Jewel and handed her the new toothbrush. I believe this was the "You had me at hello" moment in our relationship. As she got ready for bed, I prepared the couch for myself. She came out of the bathroom and said I did not have to sleep on the couch. I was waiting for her to tell me she was going home (maybe another boyfriend was waiting?). Instead she said I could share the bed with her. I was a perfect gentleman, and in the famous words of one of our presidents, "I did not have inappropriate relations" with Heather.

We continued to date and soon progressed to moving in together, getting engaged, and married. It has been over six years from that second first date, and I am even more in love with her now than I ever have been. Thank you, Sandi, for being the one responsible for me meeting my soul mate!

- Mike Paprstein

It is amazing how God works, and honestly, if my illness was what was necessary to bring two soul mates together, then I was thankful God worked through me to do it! We now have two adorable nephews, Mikey and Ian, and a beautiful niece, Olivia. I like to tease Pickle and Feather (that is our nickname for Heather). It would have been a lot easier had they met on their own instead of putting me through all I went through just so my angel nurse could marry my brother. What a blessing that the nurse who I always felt was my angel is part of our family now!

CHAPTER 14

God, Please Send Us An Angel

(Age 32)

"O LORD, you are my God; I will exalt you and praise your name, for in perfect faithfulness you have done marvelous things, things planned long ago" (Isaiah 25:1).

After all of the surgeries were behind me and my blood counts had been stable for some time, Chris, and I started discussing our options with the doctors of trying for another baby. There were mixed recommendations, but we felt our family was not complete, and we wanted to try one more time. We became pregnant (getting pregnant never seemed to be a problem for me, but holding the baby in due to my blood-clotting problem proved to be the bigger challenge). We were very excited and things were going well, but then we lost the pregnancy (the fifth one) right around eight weeks. Chris sat with me and we poured out our hearts together about everything. We were both very sad about this. Chris did not want to see me continue to go through the agony of getting my hopes up and then facing such heartbreaking disappointment. He made it clear that we needed to be thankful for the son we did have – our miracle son Tyler. I agreed, but I still felt in my heart that our family was not complete, and I believed God would grow our family somehow.

I kept having a dream about a little baby girl. It was the same dream over and over again. It was an odd dream as many can be … I was not giving birth but instead was an outsider watching the delivery. There was always the same gentleman with red hair handing me a beautiful baby girl. When I took her in my arms and looked at her angelic face, my heart was filled … our family felt complete. I would then wake up. The dream never changed, it was always the same.

I felt strongly that this last pregnancy was the baby girl I kept dreaming about, so I was crushed when we lost her. We were going to name her Samantha. My dad had come up to visit and was out in our garage. He came in looking almost spooked. I asked him what was wrong. He said, "I had this weird thing just happen. There was a vision of a little girl floating above the ground, and she looked at me and said, "Don't be sad … I'm on my way." He looked at me and said, "You are going to have a little girl in your family, trust God. I feel that was one of His angels sent to you to comfort you and to tell you not to give up hope." It put hope in my heart again, just like the dream of the angel healing me had done. I gave my dad a big hug and said, "Thanks, Dad – that is just what I needed to hear right now." As I walked back into the house, I thanked God for sending me what I needed to remind me that He was near and had a plan for us.

I prayed really hard for guidance and strength from God asking whether we should try to get pregnant again or consider looking into adoption. At the time I knew we couldn't afford an adoption. We had many medical bills from the last few years not to mention how difficult it was to adopt a baby. I continued to pray daily, remembering to be patient while believing God would guide us into His perfect will. Tyler continued to pray every day for a baby brother or sister, and he did not understand why God was not sending him one. We had to explain to him that God knows what is best for us even when we think we know better. We have to find it in our hearts to trust Him and be thankful for the blessings we already have in our lives – like each other.

CHAPTER 15

Earth Angels

(Age 34)

"And we know that in all things God works for good of those who love him, who have been called according to his purpose"
(Romans 8:28).

Mike and Heather were getting married in a week so my mom and step dad were coming in from out of town for the wedding. They had been married for years, but for some reason during this visit my step dad insisted on visiting my mom's side of the family. She looked at him and asked, "Why do you want to do that? Out of all of our trips here, you have never wanted to visit anyone other than the kids since we don't get to see them as often as we want." He couldn't explain and just said, "I'm not sure, but I think we should." So when they arrived in town, they visited my aunts as well as my cousins. My mom called me from my cousin's house. She said she thought God might be working on something for us, and I said, "What?"

She explained that when they went to visit my cousin, they found that she was taking care of three children. They started to discuss whose children they were, how they ended up with my cousin, and also that my cousin kept having a dream about a family who wanted a baby, but she kept waking up before she could figure out who that family was. One of the children was a seven-month-old baby girl named Samantha. When I heard her name, I got the chills. That was the name we were going to name our baby girl. *Could this be the baby that the little girl-angel told my dad was coming? A baby girl named Samantha to replace the one we lost?* I shook my head to come back to reality after staring off for a minute, lost in thought and in amazement at what seemed to be unfolding. Since the parents realized they would not be able to take care of three children, they loved this little baby so much they wanted my cousin to adopt her. They wanted her to have a good life, a life they knew they could not give to her, but my cousin was already in her forties and her children were grown. She loved these children but did not want to adopt the baby.

My cousin had a more than full plate. She is someone who never complains and has a heart of gold, but she had enough on her maternal plate to focus on her son and my cousin, Nick. He had been in a horrible accident when he was eighteen; he'd been hit by a semi-truck. He remained in a coma for 99 days and the family was told he would remain a vegetable. They never gave up hope! He eventually woke up from the coma, and he kept fighting and had to relearn things we all take for granted like walking, talking, and even using the restroom. He has suffered some physical affects and as a result many people think he is mentally impaired, but he is not. His mind is completely functional, but due to a limp he has and the fact that he has a condition that prevents him from speaking clearly, he is often mislabeled.

Regardless, the kid still does not give up and certainly does not want anyone feeling sorry for him! Since he cannot speak clearly, he carries a typed page of his story in his back pocket. It allows him to share it with anyone he meets. He requires an expensive surgery to correct this condition but does not have the money to pursue it. I told him not to give up his faith in God and to pray for that surgery. I always encourage him that all things are possible with God if we believe!

~~~~~~~~~

Samantha's birth mom and dad were doing everything to try and win their fight against drugs, but they kept falling prey to the addiction. Samantha was only a few months old at that time. We found out the birth mom was taking drugs throughout her pregnancy with Samantha. She mainly did heroin. Although Samantha should not have been born normal, she was born without a trace of drugs in her system or any birth defects. God had different plans for that little angel.

On Sunday we received a call from my cousin asking if we would be interested in meeting the baby. I responded immediately, "YES!" She had talked to my mom and step dad and knew we had faced many miscarriages and desperately wanted to grow our family. She had talked to the birth mom and, although she was a little hesitant, she was open to meeting us. I wanted to jump up and down but knew not to get my hopes up. I hung up trying to let it all sink in that there was a chance (even if it was small) that God could be sending us a baby. They asked if we could come over that afternoon. Chris and I discussed it and then sat Ty down to explain to him that we were going to visit my cousin, and that we would be meeting a baby that afternoon ... a baby that we MIGHT be able to adopt to be his little sister, and then we explained what adoption meant. It was all happening so fast we still had not fully absorbed it all, so we didn't expect Ty to understand. I felt like I was dreaming.

When we walked into my cousin's house and I saw that little angel, my heart immediately connected with her. She looked so sad though; she just sat in her highchair, not smiling, not holding a bottle, and not doing most things a seven-month-old baby would do. We spent some time with her, holding her and playing with her. When we left, I was sad to leave but I kept trying to shut off my heart fearing I was getting my hopes up just to have them crushed. We got into the car and Ty blurted out, "That is my baby sister!" He would not stop grinning. I explained to him that we couldn't get our hopes up because the birth parents weren't even sure they wanted her adopted by anyone other than my cousin. Ty said, "She is my sister, Mom. God answered my prayer and sent her from heaven like an angel. I feel it!" He was very sure of himself, and it broke my heart because I didn't want him to go through any more disappointments after all that he had already faced due to my health problems and the five miscarriages.

Once we got home and put Ty in bed, Chris and I sat and discussed this little angel. Chris was concerned that the drugs had most likely had a very negative impact on her, and that she may have health issues which might be difficult to handle along with my health issues. I told him I trust God, and if it ends up that we are meant to have this baby girl regardless of health issues then what a blessing it will be. He remained open to the idea, but I could tell he was guarding his heart quite a bit. I continued to pray that God would guide us.

On Wednesday of that week, my cousin called me to see if I wanted to take Samantha for an afternoon, so of course I jumped at the chance. I drove to pick her up; I still had the car seat from when Ty was a baby, so I hooked it up in the car and was off to get her. When I was strapping her into the seat she smiled at me. I called Chris when we were on our way home and told him, "Chris, I feel that she is not going back there again but will be staying with us." He said, "Honey, I know you are very excited but, please don't talk that way. You are just setting yourself up for disappointment." I heard what he was saying, but I refused to believe it because I felt that "tug" on my heart, and I knew as sure as I was sitting there that she was coming home to the home that was meant for her all along.

When I unbuckled Samantha and walked into our house with her in my arms, I cannot even explain how this little seven-month-old baby would know, but she came to life. She was so excited, smiling, bouncing in my arms as if she could not wait to get into the house she had been waiting so patiently to live in. I walked around each room of the house saying things like, "This is our living room and where we will all be spending a lot of time together as a family. This is our kitchen where Mommy cooks food for all of us." I then walked upstairs and, as soon as I turned the corner towards the bedroom that would be hers if we were able to adopt her, she started getting very excited. I walked in the room and said to her, "If God blesses us with you – this is going to be your bedroom, which is right across from your brother's room." She squealed and smiled as if she knew exactly what I had just said. I wished Chris were with me videotaping it because the reaction of this little soul was one who seemed to know she was exactly where she was supposed to be. We had a great time playing together all afternoon. I had her sitting up on a blanket in the living room, talking, playing, hugging, and kissing her. In just a few hours of giving her the extra love and attention she deserved, it was amazing to see the change in her.

I heard the garage door and knew it was Chris and Ty. Ty ran in and went straight to the restroom, not even noticing Samantha as he zipped past, but Chris walked in after him and immediately saw Samantha. They just stared at each other – as if the whole world around them stopped for this special bonding moment between a dad and his daughter. She just grinned and would not take her eyes off of him. At that very moment, I saw a bond between those two that assured me, without a doubt, that this was our baby, and she was finally home. That night my cousin called and asked if we wanted to keep her for the night. The next day she called and asked if we wanted to keep her another day, and that kept happening until the following Friday. My cousin, the lawyer, and the birth mother all came to our house to sign papers for guardianship. My step dad had gone through some hard times that caused him to pull far away from God, yet God worked through him to help us with the adoption. If he had not insisted on visiting Mom's family this trip in from Oklahoma, we would have never known about Samantha. He couldn't explain it, but he said he just *knew* they had to go. It's a powerful testimony, and you know, I believe that was an important turning point for him. He knew God had worked through him, and it changed something about him that is hard to explain.

It's amazing how God works through people to do His work, but many do not realize it because they cannot see past the messenger. Instead they are so caught up in expecting God to appear and help them that they dismiss the thought that God is all around them. It reminds me of a joke:

> There was a man called Jim who lived near a river. Jim was a very religious man.
>
> One day, the river rose over the banks and flooded the town, and Jim was forced to climb onto his porch roof. While sitting there, a man in a boat comes along and tells Jim to get in the boat with him. Jim says "No, that's okay. God

will take care of me." So the man in the boat drives off.

The water rises, so Jim climbs onto the roof of his house. Another boat comes along and the person in that one tells Jim to get in. Jim replies, "No, that's okay. God will take care of me." The person in the boat then leaves. The water rises even more, and Jim climbs onto his chimney.

Then a helicopter comes and lowers a ladder. The woman in the helicopter tells Jim to climb up the ladder and get in. Jim tells her "That's okay." The woman says, "Are you sure?" Jim says, "Yeah, I'm sure God will take care of me."

Finally, the water rises too high and Jim drowns. Jim gets up to heaven and is face-to-face with God. Jim says to God, "You told me you would take care of me! What happened?" God replied, "Well, I sent you two boats and a helicopter. What else did you want?"

- Author Unknown

It is amazing how God tries to reach us, isn't it? I felt blessed by all of those special people whom God worked through to help us. He seemed to send us exactly what and who we needed when we needed it most. One such very special person He sent our way was Teresa, one of my coworkers. She would talk to me about God and how important it was for me to be saved through Jesus. She actually is the one who taught me to pray directly to Jesus.

"Jesus answered, 'I am the way and the truth and the life. No one comes to the Father except through me'"
(John 14:6).

It was amazing the things that happened once I did exactly that. I had no idea how much God would work through Teresa even more. At a time when Chris and I were really struggling financially with a mortgage, day care expenses, and all of the medical bills, she called me and said she wanted to send us her bonus checks. I said, "Teresa, we cannot accept that. I just don't feel right about it." She would not take no for an answer and kept insisting God wanted her to do this, and she reassured me that this was how God worked. I cried thanking God for this huge blessing because we did not know how we were going to make our bills and not lose everything. He sent us just what we needed at the exact time we needed it.

God sends us everything we need, but the question is – Do we ignore His help and blessings because we are expecting God himself to appear? How many times has God tried to help us, but we have looked right past His help or turned it away because our minds have not been open to the avenues He may be using to reach us? Please open your mind and your heart to Him, and you will realize all that He is doing and trying to do in your life. When you do, the results in your life will be really powerful!

CHAPTER 16

Blessed with an Angel

(Age 35)

"And over all these virtues put on love, which binds them all together in perfect unity" (Colossians 3:14).

It would be six months before we would go to court to make the adoption final. During that time we had to be interviewed, have background checks done, and have home visits done to ensure we were fit to be adoptive parents. The timing of Dr. Sweiss coming into my life was amazing. She was able to get my blood disease into remission, which allowed my health to pass the adoption review process. Also, the entire year of surgeries I had endured was necessary, otherwise my shoulders and hips would not have been able to handle carrying around our new baby girl, Samantha. God is amazing, and His perfect timing in this situation was yet another example that despite one of the most challenging times in my life, God had a plan. I never lost faith in Him. I trusted His plan even through all of the pain and suffering, I endured facing the AVN and multiple surgeries within a year. Now He was blessing us with this angel baby. God is great!

During the past six months we had grown to love Samantha so much even though we knew she wasn't legally ours until the adoption was final. The thought of something going wrong with the adoption, thus preventing her from being our daughter, was devastating. We were nervous, and when we talked together as a family we realized that Satan had planted the idea in all of our heads that we could lose her. Those thoughts were overwhelming at times, especially in the weeks leading up to the adoption. During our drive to the courtroom, worry and anxiety were building in all of us. What would our family do if she was taken from us? I started getting knots in my stomach but knew we had to trust God and His plan. I silently prayed, *Jesus, please be with us as we walk into the courtroom today. Take all of this anxiety and worry, which Satan has planted, and replace it with peace and trust in you, Lord. Amen.*

The courtroom was the first time we were meeting the birth dad. As you know, we had already met Samantha's birth mom. When we walked into the courtroom, I was in awe of God, once again. I couldn't believe what I was seeing – there, in front of us, stood the red-haired man from my dream, the one who handed me the angel baby! At that moment, peace radiated my soul. I felt God take each step with me as our family, including Tyler, approached the bench. God reminded me not to worry about anything but to give my worries to Him. He was in control of our lives – not Satan, not the courts … *only God*. He would not forsake us if we believed in Him and trusted His plan.

"When anxiety was great within me, your consolation
brought joy to my soul" (Psalm 94:19).

The adoption day turned out to be one of the best days of our lives. The lawyer said that in twenty years of doing adoptions he had never seen an adoption that was as meant to be as this one. Both birth parents showed up in court to sign the papers and make it official. Every single thing that needed to fall into place DID, not to mention that the whole adoption was done for less than $5,000.

Tyler was right! God answered his prayer and sent us our angel, Samantha. It was as if she fell out of the sky when our hearts needed her most. We had her picture taken in wings so we could include a picture of our little angel in the adoption announcement. Our hearts were filled when she came into our lives. We cannot imagine life without her in it. It feels so right and so perfect, like she was meant to be part of our family from the moment she was conceived. Despite the odds against her of the drugs her birth mom had taken while Samantha was in the womb, she was born without a trace of drugs in her system. She is a thriving, healthy, and beautiful girl who looks like a true angel. Her blonde curls and blue eyes draw people to her. I find that every time we are out people stop us to say how beautiful she is.

"I prayed for this child, and the Lord has granted me
what I asked of Him" (1 Samuel 1:27).

As soon as Samantha came into our lives in 2003, our family felt complete. I did not have any major health issues for a couple of years. It was a great gift to be able to spend time bonding as a family without worrying about any health issues, which was quite a change from what we were used to, but God knew our family needed that time. We were blessed He gave us that time as a family. There was a time when I had prayed just to have one day to feel well, so when I was blessed with a couple of years, I knew what a gift I'd been given.

Health problems can be overwhelming for anyone, no matter what your age, but don't let them discourage you. Open up your heart to God and know He is there so you are not facing it alone. And never forget that even if you stop searching for Him, He will find you!

Father John Powell, a Professor at Loyola University in Chicago, writes about a student in his Theology of Faith class named Tommy:

Finding God

> Some twelve years ago, I stood watching my
> university students file into the classroom for
> our first session in the Theology of Faith. That
> was the day I first saw Tommy. My eyes and my
> mind both blinked. He was combing his long
> flaxen hair, which hung six inches below his
> shoulders. It was the first time I had ever seen
> a boy with hair that long. I guess it was just
> coming into fashion then. I know in my mind
> that it isn't what's on your head but what's in
> it that counts; but on that day I was unprepared

and my emotions flipped. I immediately filed Tommy under "S" for strange ... Very strange.

Tommy turned out to be the "atheist in residence" in my Theology of Faith course. He constantly objected to, smirked at, or whined about the possibility of an unconditionally loving Father/God. We endured each other in relative peace for one semester, although I admit he was for me, at times, a serious pain in the back pew.

When he came up at the end of the course to turn in his final exam, he asked in a cynical tone, "Do you think I'll ever find God?" I decided instantly on a little shock therapy. "No!" I said very emphatically. "Why not?" he responded. "I thought that was the product you were pushing."

I let him get five steps from the classroom door and then called out, "Tommy! I don't think you'll ever find Him, but I am absolutely certain that He will find you!" He shrugged a little and left my class and my life. I felt slightly disappointed at the thought that he had missed my clever line – He will find you! At least I thought it was clever.

Later I heard that Tommy had graduated, and I was duly grateful. Then a sad report came. I heard that Tommy had terminal cancer. Before I could search him out, he came to see me. When he walked into my office, his body was very badly wasted and the long hair had all fallen out as a result of chemotherapy. But his eyes were bright and his voice was firm, for the first time, I believe.

"Tommy, I've thought about you so often; I hear you are sick," I blurted out.

"Oh, yes, very sick. I have cancer in both lungs. It's a matter of weeks."

"Can you talk about it, Tom?" I asked.

"Sure, what would you like to know?" he replied.

"What's it like to be only twenty-four and dying?"

"Well, it could be worse."

"Like what?"

"Well, like being fifty and having no values or ideals, like being fifty and thinking that booze, seducing women, and making money are the real biggies in life." I began to look through my mental file cabinet under "S" where I had filed Tommy as strange. (It seems as though everybody I try to reject by classification, God sends back into my life to educate me.)

"But what I really came to see you about," Tom said, "is something you said to me on the last day of class." (He remembered!) He continued, "I asked you if you thought I would ever find God, and you said, 'No!' which surprised me. Then you said, 'But He will find you.' I thought about that a lot, even though my search for God was hardly intense at that time. (My clever line – he thought about that a lot!)

"But when the doctors removed a lump from my groin and told me that it was malignant, that's when I got serious about locating God. And when the malignancy spread into my vital organs, I really began banging bloody fists against the bronze doors of heaven. But God

did not come out. In fact, nothing happened.
Did you ever try anything for a long time
with great effort and with no success? You get
psychologically gutted, fed up with trying. And
then you quit Well, one day, I woke up, and
instead of throwing a few more futile appeals
over that high brick wall to a God who may be
or may not be there, I just quit. I decided that I
didn't really care about God, about an afterlife,
or anything like that. I decided to spend what
time I had left doing something more profitable.
I thought about you and your class, and I
remembered something else you had said: 'The
essential sadness is to go through life without
loving. But it would be almost equally sad to go
through life and leave this world without ever
telling those you loved that you had loved them.'
So, I began with the hardest one, my dad. He
was reading the newspaper when I approached
him. 'Dad.' 'Yes, what?' he asked without
lowering the newspaper.

'Dad, I would like to talk with you.' 'Well, talk.'
'I mean, it's really important.' The newspaper
came down three slow inches. 'What is it?'
'Dad, I love you; I just wanted you to know
that.'" Tom smiled at me and said it with
obvious satisfaction, as though he felt a warm
and secret joy flowing inside of him.

"The newspaper fluttered to the floor. Then my
father did two things I could never remember
him ever doing before. He cried, and he hugged
me. We talked all night, even though he had to
go to work the next morning. It felt so good to
be close to my father, to see his tears, to feel his
hug, to hear him say that he loved me. It was
easier with my mother and little brother. They
cried with me, too, and we hugged each other

and started saying real nice things to each other. We shared the things we had been keeping secret for so many years.

"I was only sorry about one thing — that I had waited so long. Here I was, just beginning to open up to all the people I had actually been close to.

"Then one day I turned around and God was there. He didn't come to me when I pleaded with Him. I guess I was like an animal trainer holding out a hoop saying 'C'mon, jump through. C'mon, I'll give you three days, three weeks.' Apparently God does things in His own way and at His own hour. But the important thing is that He was there. He found me! You were right. He found me, even after I stopped looking for Him."

"Tommy," I practically gasped, "I think you are saying something very important and much more universal than you realize. To me, at least, you are saying that the surest way to find God is not to make Him a private possession, a problem solver, or an instant consolation in time of need, but rather by opening to love. You know, the Apostle John said that. He said: 'God is love, and anyone who lives in love is living with God and God is living in him.' Tom, could I ask you a favor? You know, when I had you in class you were a real pain. But (laughingly) you can make it all up to me now. Would you come into my present Theology of Faith course and tell them what you have just told me? If I told them the same thing it wouldn't be half as effective as if you were to tell it."

"Oooh, I was ready for you, but I don't know if I'm ready for your class."

"Tom, think about it. If and when you are ready, give me a call."

In a few days Tom called and said he was ready for the class, that he wanted to do that for God and for me. So we scheduled a date.

However, he never made it. He had another appointment, far more important than the one with me and my class. Of course, his life was not really ended by his death, only changed. He made the great step from faith into vision. He found a life far more beautiful than the eye of man has ever seen or the ear of man has ever heard or the mind of man has ever imagined.

Before he died, we talked one last time.

"I'm not going to make it to your class," he said.

"I know, Tom."

"Will you tell them for me? Will you ... tell the whole world for me?"

"I will, Tom. I'll tell them. I'll do my best."

So, to all of you who have been kind enough to read this simple story about God's love, thank you for listening. And to you, Tommy, somewhere in the sunlit, verdant hills of heaven – I told them, Tommy, as best I could.

If this story means anything to you, please pass it on to a friend or two. It is a true story and is not enhanced for publicity purposes.

With thanks,
Rev. John Powell,
Professor, Loyola University[5]

CHAPTER 17

Trust in Him

(Age 37)

"The Lord is a refuge for the oppressed, a stronghold in time of trouble. Those who know your name will trust in you, for you, Lord, have never forsaken those who seek you" (Psalm 9:9-10).

"Honey, I know this is an odd request, but do you feel a lump right here?" I said to Chris as I pointed to an area on the outside of my right breast. Being the loving husband that he is, he didn't even think twice about walking over to see if he felt a lump. He said, "Not really, why?" I looked at him with a puzzled look and said, "I am not sure. I thought I felt a lump, but now I don't. Something keeps telling me that I need to have a mammogram. I've actually felt like this for a few months but haven't taken the time to do anything since things have been so busy with the kids and both of us traveling for work and all." He walked over to give me a hug and said, "You need to make an appointment then if you are worried about it, but I'm sure everything is going to be fine." I shrugged my shoulders and tried convincing myself that since he didn't feel a lump I was sure I was worrying about nothing.

A few weeks passed by, and I kept feeling like I needed to get it checked out. Although I didn't have a good reason to request a mammogram other than my heart tugging me to, I called and made an appointment with my gynecologist. When I saw her, I explained that sometimes I could feel lumps in my right breast, but then they would go away. "Yes, that is completely normal, especially if it is around your ovulation cycle." the doctor said. I looked at her and said, "I can't explain why, maybe due to my health history, I guess, but I feel like I need to have a mammogram." She could tell by the look on my face that I really felt I needed to get one to check things out. She told me generally they do not recommend mammograms until forty years of age, but she thought it was a good idea due to my history. I was scheduled to have the mammogram a couple of weeks later.

~~~~~~~~~

"Sandra Rauwolf," the nurse said into the waiting room calling me back for my mammogram. I followed the nurse back and changed into the hospital gown that she had draped over the chair before she left the room. The technician came into the room and explained the tests she was going to be doing. She was very nice and brought me close to the machine so that she could position me properly for the test. The technician took quite a few pictures of each breast and told me the doctor would be calling me in a week to discuss the results. "Thank you," I said to her as she walked out the door and pulled it closed behind her. I got dressed and thought, *This wasn't bad at all.* I was a little worried when I had heard what they would have to do to get the pictures. I'll just say I heard it wasn't fun and nothing you would stand in line to do! So as I walked past the reception desk, I was smiling. I had a little jump in my step feeling silently proud that I had survived my first mammogram! It was not bad at all.

The following week the doctor called me and told me they saw a cyst in my left breast, but it looked completely normal. She recommended a follow-up mammogram in a year due to the immunosuppressive medicines I have to take. Immunosuppressive drugs come along with the risks of developing cancer, especially the one particular medicine I was taking.

"See, I told you all would be fine," Chris said to me as he smiled. I looked at him with that look that said, *I am still not convinced*, and he said, "What? What is the matter?" I looked up at him and said, "I don't know, I just feel that is not good enough. I feel it needs to be checked out more." I called Dr. Sweiss and explained to her that I'd like to have a follow-up mammogram done soon at the University of Chicago, although I had just had one. She was wonderful as usual and listened to my concerns. She agreed that we should evaluate the cyst they found a little bit further. An appointment was made for me the next month to see a doctor in the Breast Clinic at University of Chicago.

The doctor examined me and sent me down the hall to have the mammogram done. After the test, the technician brought me back to the room so the doctor could review the results with me. The doctor said the left cyst they saw did look normal, but he wanted to have an ultrasound done to ensure everything was okay. The nurse escorted me into the ultrasound room. I had never heard of an ultrasound of the breast. Anyway, I lay back on the examining table while the technician prepared the ultrasound wand with a warm, jelly-like ointment. He then did an ultrasound of the cyst they saw in my left breast. The cyst showed blood flow going to it, which was a bit odd. Typically cysts did not have blood flow going to them like mine showed.

At my request, the breast specialist paged my doctor to discuss the findings with him. He is not only a hematologist but also an oncologist, one who had followed my case for years and is highly respected in his field. I did not want anything (particularly anything that could be related to cancer) done without it being discussed with him first. They decided it would be best to remove the cyst using a procedure called a lumpectomy. A lumpectomy is a common surgery for breast cancer where it removes the lump and the surrounding tissues. "Wow, another surgery?" I said as I shook my head. He said, "Yes, but it is not an invasive surgery so it should be much easier than your others." However, he explained that it was still considered major surgery and that I would be going under anesthesia for the procedure. I was beginning to think God put me on this earth to fund the medical field, particularly the surgeons and the anesthesiologists. *Alright then, let's help another team of doctors earn their paychecks!* I thought. I knew all of the risks involved with surgery, so although he had to share them with me, I had become all too familiar with surgery and the risks that came along with it. Well, I was at least "trying" to listen with a smile.

My surgery was scheduled for November. Somehow the timing of my surgeries or health episodes seemed to fall around the holidays or early spring, particularly March! Due to an acquisition of our company a year prior, my new co-workers were not privy to the health problems I had faced years previous – thank goodness! My health had improved dramatically. It allowed me to go back to work full-time and even travel to the corporate headquarters in Yardley, PA for quarterly visits. I was leading a normal life – a life of health; a life filled with people at work who knew me for me and not my disease. I had new friends and new close girlfriends in addition to all of the wonderful people God had already blessed me with. I felt like I had been given a fresh start in life.

I got a little overwhelmed when I left the doctor's office because all of my health issues from years ago came flooding back as if they had happened yesterday. I wasn't ready to share this part of my life with my new co-workers, my new friends, or my new boss. I wanted only to have this life that was so normal and so wonderful without losing my identity to my health issues again. Some would love attention like this, but I'd had more than my share of attention over the years, and it was the last thing I wanted.

I knew the chances were high that it could be cancer because of the immunosuppressive medications I had been on. However, I have to say I have no regrets about taking those, no matter what the outcome, because they helped give me my life back. I decided I needed to share what I was going through with those I was closest to at work. After all, I would need a good support system at home and work if I was diagnosed with cancer, right? It was a difficult decision to make. If they knew all of the surgeries and everything I had been through, they would know the last thing I wanted was attention from this, so I was glad they didn't know.

Although I was nervous about it, my next trip into the office, I had made plans to explain to each of my coworkers and good friends what was ahead for me. I prayed that God would be with me, because I knew it would be difficult opening up about some of my health issues, and that because of it, I may lose some friendships. I'd had some friends who couldn't handle it all very well through the years and so they had distanced themselves from my friendship. Some of the new friendships I had gained in my new job were very close to my heart, as if I had known them my whole life, so the thought of any of them distancing themselves from me was difficult to bear. I also did not want them to look at me differently and see me only for my health issues. If I just didn't have to have surgery, I could have kept this entire health thing to myself.

However, along this incredible, spiritual journey, it had become more and more obvious to me that there is a reason for everything. I had a choice; I could try to keep it private, but I also realized how much we need the support of others – especially those we care about. God places people around us and works through them to support and love us during difficult times. Sometimes we may even find God in a stranger offering advice to guide us along our path, but we have to be open to it and what God is doing in our lives at the time. I trusted God in this situation, and the support and love I felt from my new friends and coworkers was incredible. I felt very blessed indeed!

My doctors had been wondering about the possibility of my having cancer for some time due to spots found in my lungs years ago. For years they had been monitoring the spots through regular lung CT scans looking for any type of change. Other patients would have gone through a lung biopsy as soon as the results of the first lung scan came back, but there were too many risks involved with me, especially due to the blood clotting issues. I talked to Dr. Sweiss about the lump found in my breast and my concerns. She assured me all would be fine and explained that the location of this being in my breast couldn't be a more ideal spot. The lumpectomy went well. The surgeon said it would take about a week for the results.

~~~~~~~~~~~

The first week everyone was patient while waiting for the results – well, as patient as we could be, except for Tyler. A few days after I had been home from the hospital, Ty walked in the door from school, and before he said hi, he blurted out, "Mom, did the doctor call about your surgery results yet?" He had such worry on his face that it broke my heart. He was eleven years old at the time and understood the word cancer. After he lost his Grandpa Gene to stomach cancer, any time he heard that someone had cancer, he worried tremendously and thought it meant certain death.

I can remember it so clearly. He stood there trying to stand tall and be strong but his eyes started filling up with tears. He was doing everything to stop the tears, but they welled in his eyes. He looked at me and said, "Mom, I can't ever lose you. I need you here. I love Dad and everything, but I need you. You help me through so many things. Please don't leave me, Mom – please." It took every ounce of strength I had not to fall apart because I could feel the pain flowing right from his heart directly into mine. I hugged him tightly and cried, not because of what I was facing, but because of what it was doing to my family. If only each of them could have the same peace I had inside that comes from totally trusting God. It is not easy, but in the moments when you do trust Him completely, there is no other feeling like it in the world. While wiping tears from his face and mine, I said, "Ty, don't worry. We will get through this, honey. We have to trust God and His plans no matter what they may be. Let's focus on the blessings of all of this." He looked at me like I was crazy. I could tell he was thinking, *How can you find something good in a situation that could take you away from me? You're my mother and I need you!* I continued, "This surgery is one that will allow them to safely do a biopsy where other areas they wanted to biopsy weren't safe enough for me. The results of this may give the doctors the answers they need to cure me forever. We don't know what God has ahead but let's trust Him, okay honey?" He looked at me with worry still in his eyes, so I grabbed him for another hug, a long one. I silently prayed, *Jesus, please give us the strength to face whatever is ahead. My family struggles deeply, especially since they are still learning how to trust You completely. Please hear my prayer and bring them peace ... bring them You. Amen.* I hugged him for a few moments longer, not wanting to let go.

A couple of weeks passed by and still there were no biopsy results. I was receiving a lot of phone calls and emails from family and friends asking about the results. It meant a lot to me how much people cared. The thing that filled my soul was that in the midst of these challenges and waiting for "the news," those calls provided me another reason to share my belief and trust in God with each one who expressed concern for me. I will not deny, though, that everyone was going through a true test of faith during this waiting period, including me! I prayed for strength and asked God not to let my faith falter. It was difficult to sit and watch what it was doing to those around me who still struggled with their faith so much. I kept praying and trusting that somehow all we were going through would bring them closer to God, just as it had done for me. They just were not there yet. Each day seemed like a week. After the first week when we still had not heard anything, each day started to feel like a month. I kept praying for those around me as well as for myself. We needed to stay strong and not lose sight of Him.

A few weeks after the surgery, my doctor called with the results. He said, "Sandi, I don't know what it is with you, it seems you are always the rarity, but the results had to be sent out to Mayo Clinic to confirm the diagnosis so it has taken longer than normal. The cyst in your breast showed MALT lymphoma, and this type of lymphoma only manifests in the breast in approximately 1% of patients." Boy if I only played the lotto with these odds I'd be a millionaire five times over! "MALT Lymphoma? What does this mean for me?" I asked him. He said he was not sure, but that he would have to run some additional tests before he could determine what treatments would be best for me.

My dad happened to be there at the time I got this phone call. He has always struggled with my illness and how difficult it was watching me almost lose my life to it a few times. He worried constantly, so I have always tried to encourage him by telling him we have to give our worries to God and trust we are going through things for a reason. Now that I am a mother, I understand how his heart must feel. I can only imagine the agony I would feel watching my oldest child face a life-threatening illness, and how overwhelming would be the thought of possibly losing him. Again, in times like this when we feel so overwhelmed, so worried, so lost – we CAN do something. We can pray, and we can trust God!

"What is it, Sandi? What did he say?" my dad asked with great worry on his face – so much worry that I didn't want to tell him, but I did. I explained that they had found a lymphoma. The look on his face was as if he had just lost his best friend. I said to him, "Dad, it is all going to be fine. Please don't worry! God did not bring me this far to have this happen. Give me a few minutes to research it." I went over to my computer and read multiple articles on MALT lymphoma. I shared with my dad how this particular type looked like the best one to have because it was the most treatable of all of the lymphomas. I saw the worry on his face lift a bit. He said, "But it is still cancer, Sandi." I looked at him and said, "I know, Dad, but does it really matter? I have God on my side, and He will decide the plan for my life." He just sat there shaking his head because despite his faith, he always seemed to be amazed at exactly how strong mine was and how I trusted God in all of the things that I faced – things he said he could never imagine having the strength to face himself.

~~~~~~~~

Multiple tests were ordered including a PET scan to see if the lymphoma had spread to any other part of my body. A PET scan is a test used to detect cancer. I was injected with a radioactive substance and then asked to wait approximately thirty minutes while it worked its way through my system (basically into my tissues). I was then placed on a cushioned table that slides into a doughnut-shaped machine that would scan my body for cancer. The odds were against me because it is very rare that MALT lymphoma starts in the breast, so there was probably another originating source of the cancer. I think everyone, including the doctors, was expecting the tests to show the lymphoma had spread throughout my body.

I found my faith being tested again as I waited for the results. I knew if the results showed cancer throughout my body that my purpose here on earth may be done. I had made peace with that a few years ago because I believe heaven is a much better place than anything life here on earth can offer. However, what I found myself struggling with was the thought of leaving my children behind without a mother. I prayed as tears streamed down my face, *What about them, Jesus? What about them? Please help me to trust Your plan with everything, because the thought of leaving my children and the pain it would cause them is too much for me to bear at times. Give me strength. I am trusting in You. Amen.* I knew that no matter what the results showed, God would decide when it was my time to depart this earth, not any test result or any doctor. I prayed and believed that despite the odds, God would send me another wonderful blessing that I could share as a testimony to what is possible through Him. It seemed the tension in our house could be cut with a knife. Any time I talked to my parents they were worried about me. My children, particularly Tyler, were having a very difficult time knowing their mom had cancer and could possibly die. I felt peace inside but had my weak moments where I let things build up because I always tried to be strong for everyone around me. I carried this incredible weight on my shoulders seeing what my health issues did to those who cared for me. If I could only take the peace and faith from my heart and put it into theirs, it would be awesome – that was all I wanted for them … peace, the peace that is only possible with God.

My follow-up appointment to discuss the test results went great!! We were very thankful to hear that the scan was within normal ranges. "Praise, God!!" I shouted with joy. The doctor said we had one more test to get through because MALT lymphoma often starts with its source in the gastrointestinal area. A biopsy was ordered to rule that out. One down, one to go – we can do this! I had the GI biopsies done, and we were blessed again; each of those biopsies showed no sign of MALT lymphoma. It appeared the lymphoma had been contained and no chemotherapy or radiation was necessary at that time. We were very thankful for this gift. God had sent another big blessing our way! It was absolutely amazing!

God continued to prove that when we believe in Him, anything is possible. Tyler was so happy when I told him, he just hugged me for what seemed like forever. "Ty, this is an important life lesson to trust God with all things and never, ever give up hope. He has sent us another blessing; isn't that wonderful?" I said to him as I held him. My heart was filled with so much love and faith. The best way to describe it is in the words of our beautiful four-year-old daughter, Samantha: "My heart feels fluffy, Mommy." Fluffy – what a great way to describe a perfect heart, one so filled with God that it is completely weightless!

What a blessing that before the lymphoma could take over my body, it presented in such a rare but safe place that it could easily be removed – a place that also happened to be one of *the* safest biopsies for me due to my complicated health history. It was so safe that my doctors felt the benefits outweighed the risks and allowed the surgery. Had it presented anywhere else, by the time they would have found it, it would have most likely been in advanced stages, but this MALT lymphoma presented in my breast – yes, which happens in only one percent of patients, but those odds allowed them to safely perform the biopsy and provide a diagnosis that could save my life. This diagnosis gave me the chance to be proactive in fighting a cancer that can turn aggressive very quickly and thus become difficult to treat, which would then reduce the odds of survival. The doctors now know to monitor me for the signs of lymphoma because early treatment in such a condition is critical.

I could have easily focused on the negative instead of trusting God's plan for my life. I knew all things happen for a reason and not to question things like, "Why me out of all of the patients in the world (1%) would have MALT lymphoma in my breast? Why couldn't it just be a cyst like the majority of women have?" I focused on whatever good was going to come out of it all. Whenever I found myself getting weak (even the strongest believers have weak moments), I let God carry me. I kept my faith and knew exactly how blessed I was being in the small percentage of patients where it presented in the breast.

God is amazing; I felt yet again like I had hit the lottery!! His continual blessings seemed too good to be true!

Who would have known that little "Miss Positive Mental Attitude" from years ago would have grown that attitude into an even stronger one as a result of the seed God had first planted deep in my heart and that grew roots to ensure it stayed strong and then slowly bloomed throughout this incredible journey into a beautiful flower containing multiple petals ... faith, belief, trust, strength, perseverance, love, compassion, empathy, peace, and happiness, all surrounding the magnificent center which was God. Attitude is so important, and with God we can have a great attitude, can't we? Through God we can have an indescribable peace, and when we welcome Him into our hearts our perspective changes forever in a very powerful way. We become the good finders because we look for the good in all situations. If you are not a believer, I encourage you to believe in Him so you can have a life filled with so much it is beyond comprehension. Your perspective alone is worth its weight in gold because it will find the blessings in every situation, even the darkest of them.

CHAPTER 18

New Beginnings

(Age 38)

"Praise be to the Lord, for he has heard my cry for mercy. The Lord is my strength and my shield; my heart trusts in him, and I am helped. My heart leaps for joy and I will give thanks to him in song" (Psalm 28:6-7).

It seems throughout our years of marriage, March always presented itself with challenges – particularly health issues for me. March 2007 was no different from any other year. Chris and I found ourselves taking a step back in order to also take a deep breath and say, "Did that all really just happen?" March Madness has its own meaning in the Rauwolf household, that is for sure! Every year for some time now it seems there is something major we face in March. I am beginning to wonder if it is meant to bring a reminder of "new beginnings" in the spring ensuring our focus is where it is supposed to be in life instead of getting caught up in the rat race we know we can all get pulled into daily.

My health had been very stable, and we were once again in the midst of running in a bunch of different directions with our jobs and with the kids' activities, but we were blessed nonetheless for all of it. I then became ill quite suddenly. It started out as abdominal pain and discomfort, but it quickly turned into full abdominal distention (swelling) with vomiting and a fever. It seemed I had caught a pretty horrible flu virus that had no mercy whatsoever on my intestines. I wasn't able to eat any solid foods for days. First I was not able to hold anything down, then I started to feel a little better a couple of days later when my body would begin craving food but yet making it a known fact that it wanted nothing to do with it! Any solid food caused horrible pain and gassiness. I felt again like I had years ago where I was the "blueberry girl" because I was so bloated. I felt like saying, *Would someone just put a pin in me so I can feel better?* We did not know what was going on but suspected the flu was causing my blood disease to kick into full-attack mode, as was usually the case.

As I lay there quite ill, I kept checking for the normal signs of my blood disease activating (i.e. jaundice, shortness of breath), but my color was pale as happens with anyone who has the flu. "Chris, I feel so sick – this flu is absolutely horrible," I said to my husband after a couple of days of being in bed. I kept praying every day that I would get a little better and that God would relieve this pain from my stomach – *What a strong flu it is indeed!* I thought. A couple of days later, I tried once again to introduce solid foods but my body wanted no part of it. The good news was that my stomach was half the size it had been a couple of days ago. I had looked about six months pregnant earlier that week.

I tried to muster up some energy to take a bath but couldn't do it without help. "Honey, would you please help me with a bath? I know I am still sick, but I feel gross, and I think a warm bath might help me feel better," I said to Chris when he came upstairs to check on me. God bless him! He has taken such good care of me – all without ever complaining. He was working all day, and then coming home and taking care of the kids, me, and everything else in the house.

"No problem. Give me a few minutes to clean up after dinner and get the kids settled," he said. Boy did this bring back memories to almost ten years ago when Chris had to give me baths, dress me, and take care of my every need because I was so ill. I prayed, *Jesus, please hear my prayer and heal me. I am so thankful for the health You have given me the last few years. The thought of going back to a life of being ill again is more than I can bear at this time. Please hear my prayer. I believe in You and Your healing powers. Amen.*

Sitting on the edge of our whirlpool tub, I knew I had to go to the hospital. I could hardly breathe again, just like years ago. Tears rolled down my face. "Jesus, I don't want to go back to a life of being sick. Please help me, please see me through this and make me well again," I prayed aloud through my tears. I felt my stomach hurting but not from the flu; instead, it was from worry. I knew I had to give all of these worries to God and trust Him, but I was having a weak moment. The thought of going into a five-year spiral of being ill was overwhelming. I saw the look on Chris' face and knew he felt the same way. He handed me the phone so that I could page Dr. Sweiss. She called me within fifteen minutes – what a great doctor I was blessed with! I explained to her what had been going on the last few days. I was hoping she would say that I should wait one more day to see if my body would fight off the flu, but her voice on the other end made it clear I needed to get to the ER soon, particularly with the type of flu viruses that were circulating that year. Even healthy individuals without rare blood disorders were having difficult times fighting off these new sets of viruses. She said, "With you, we cannot take any chances."

So the flurry of calls and plans began. Our family and friends were wonderful and jumped in to save the day yet again for us. Grandpa Ted came up to watch the kids, Aunt Carrie was on call for anything we needed, not to mention we knew all of the rest of our family and friends would have been there at the drop of a hat if we needed anything else at all. We are incredibly blessed!!! I hugged the kids tightly and told them I loved them and not to worry, but that the flu was making me pretty sick, and I needed to go to the hospital to get better. I saw the worry in Ty's eyes. This was something he was all too familiar with, but fortunately nothing he had faced since he was Samantha's age.

I found myself looking into Samantha's eyes flashing back to the life we faced when Ty was her age (four years old) and remembering the countless trips to the ER with no treatment working, wondering if we were about to start that roller coaster ride yet again. My heart broke as we pulled out of the driveway; I turned and looked at my two precious kids with a forced smile and a wave, assuring them that "Mom was going to be okay."

We got to the ER at University of Chicago, and it was quite busy as usual. They are faced often with major traumas including gunshot wounds, major accidents with "life" flights going in and out constantly. Chris and I were prepared to sit and wait for hours until I could be seen, since patients are evaluated and taken by severity of symptoms. I sat patiently waiting for the triage nurse to evaluate me. I could barely walk at this time and my heart was racing out of my chest. I couldn't help but think *this is what I deserve for not taking the time yet again to get a flu shot. When will I ever learn!*

The nurse called me back, took my vitals, and looked at me with worry and concern. My heart rate was over 120 BPM. A normal heart rate average is from 60 to 85 beats per minute. Mine was double the normal rate! She performed what is called a "bedside" blood count and found that my hemoglobin had dropped to critical levels; it was 4.7 with normal levels being from 12 to 16. My hematocrit was around 15, and that should have been between 34 and 46. If I am calculating correctly, my body was about five units low on blood. The last time my counts were this low I was immediately admitted to ICU and the doctors were giving me six units of blood at the same time.

They rushed me back to the ER and started taking multiple tubes of blood to properly cross-match me for blood transfusions. The challenge was that I am a very hard one to cross-match. My blood type is AB+ (one of the rare ones), and due to the numerous blood transfusions I'd had in years past, my body had built up many antibodies against the blood, and thus it could take at least twenty-four hours to find a match for me. I thought, "Do we have twenty-four hours?"

My disease is extremely complicated and sensitive to the slightest change. It appeared my disease was in high-active state, which meant my body was aggressively attacking and killing my red blood cells. That means that any introduction of new blood (once they could finally find a match) could be killed off as quickly as it was given to me. Since my blood counts were already critical, the question was whether we should introduce a blood transfusion. The introduction of blood could cause my body to form a full-force attack on all of the red blood cells, including the new blood and my existing blood. There was no room at all for chance because any more destruction of cells could be fatal.

I sat there praying. This time I was truly scared. Despite my strong faith at that moment, I was definitely aware that I am only human. Even though I knew God was by my side every step of the way, I was still scared. If I felt this way, I knew Chris had to have been dying inside. I could see the pain and worry in his face. The doctors were scrambling, paging my doctors, and gathering all of the specifics of this complicated case that had just come in the door. I was started on IV steroids immediately, which generally is what controls any kind of crisis for me. It suppresses the immune system in hopes of preventing my body from so aggressively killing off my red blood cells. My gut was telling me this was not the normal crash ... although it had been years (thank goodness) since I had faced anything like this, I know my body all too well, and this was definitely different.

After a few hours in the ER and going through numerous tests, I was admitted to a private room with blood transfusions ready for bedside administration so they could closely monitor me. It appeared all of my blood counts were critical, not just my red cells. The doctor came in and said, "Sandi your blood counts are very concerning. Your white blood cell count is extremely high at 50,000 (normal is 5,000 - 11,000). We are not sure if it is related to your lymphoma diagnosis found in 2005."

Chris turned and looked at me very concerned. "Does this mean the cancer has spread?" I asked.

"We are not sure until we run more tests. Your platelets are only 17,000, and they are supposed to be between 130,000 and 400,000," the doctor explained. We knew since my platelets were low that things were now even more complicated because on top of everything else, the risk of internal bleeding was in the mix. I found myself getting overwhelmed at all of the news. It was yet another roller coaster ride just like years ago. One minute we would be told something that was pretty hard to hear and then, just as we were absorbing that, we would find out another thing. I did my best to hold it together for my husband and knew I had to trust God. It had been years since I had been this sick, and after feeling well for so long I was petrified of having my normal life yanked out from under me again.

Please give me strength to endure whatever is ahead, I prayed. The doctors ordered an additional chest/abdomen CT scan. I had to gulp down the contrast liquid hoping I could keep it down for them to capture the image they needed. They were questioning whether I had clots in my organs, despite the blood thinner I had been taking for years (since the major episode I had in 1998). They also wanted to see if the lymphoma had spread and taken over my abdomen ... neither being good news.

They came to take me down for the lung/abdominal scan. Chris saw the worry on my face as I left my room. He didn't see the normal "all is going to be fine, honey" face that I usually had despite challenges of this type. I was wheeled down alone to get my scan. I felt anxiety building up the closer we got to the radiology area of the hospital. It got to be too much, so I closed my eyes and prayed very hard ... *Jesus, I cannot do this alone. I need you with me. I am scared! Hear my prayer and let me know you are here. Amen.*

At that moment the feeling that went through my soul was like no other. A wondrous sense of peace come over me that was so calming it was indescribable; it was as if someone had surrounded me with an embrace. I could almost hear Someone whisper, "I am here and all is going to be fine … trust me." My worries, fears, and anxieties were gone at that very moment! I had my test and came back to the room smiling ear-to-ear. Chris looked at me and said, "What in the world has gotten into you – did they give you some good pain medications for the test or something?" I hugged him and said, "All is going to be fine. I am so excited to see what God is doing with all of this now. Something really good is going to come out of it ... another chapter for my book." He smiled but still struggled with that whole concept. He believed in God but did not understand why God kept putting me through all of this. He was still struggling with turning to God for help or strength.

Results of the scan showed large amounts of fluid in my abdomen and a mass on my right ovary. Dr. Sweiss was talking to the top ovarian cancer experts at the University of Chicago. All of the fluid in my abdomen caused a major alert that the lymphoma could be active or, even worse, that I was facing advanced stage ovarian cancer. It was not exactly the news we wanted to hear but after that feeling of peace which had come over me, I knew God was with me and all was going to be fine. Dr. Sweiss called me that night just to check on me because she knew what all of these test results were indicating, but she wanted to know how I was feeling about it. I think she felt my struggles from earlier in the day. "All will be great," I told her, "and no matter what the outcome is, God has a plan here, and I am excited to be part of it. I have to trust Him." She understood because she knows how important faith is in all parts of our lives – the good and the bad, the ups and the downs, just like the issues I had faced throughout the years.

She is an amazing doctor and, without a doubt, I feel she is guided by the Holy Spirit in her practice. She has a presence about her that truly is like an angel. She has tried unique treatments that some doctors may question, like the Cell Cept for my blood disorder, but those treatments have worked! God knows what is best and will guide those who are open to His guidance. As a result she has saved the lives of many patients, including mine. Imagine the type of treatment all patients could receive if medical doctors would combine spirituality and medicine. I trust God is going to have her do something big in this life, and she is going to help many more patients. She already did something very big in my life when God sent her to be my doctor. God worked through her to heal me, and thus she saved my life just like in my dream.

Dr. Sweiss and I discussed how everyone had been praying for a miracle. It brought tears to her eyes thinking of me, my family, and my children because of what seemed to be obvious signs that things were *not* going to be okay for me. Despite the outlook and medical results, we didn't give up hope or faith that God would guide her yet again in my treatment. We all continued to pray for a miracle believing He would answer our prayers.

The next day, a follow-up ultrasound and examination from the gynecology team showed that there was fluid in my abdomen. Before any type of treatment could be started, they would need to obtain some of the fluid around the ovary, but there were too many risks of me bleeding since my platelets were low. They also suspected I had bled internally due to an ovarian cyst that had burst one week prior. A burst cyst had been filling my abdomen with blood for days while I lay there thinking I had the flu! My doctor started a new treatment of steroids and a combination of other medications I had taken before. My counts started to come up every day without any transfusions being required. I was released from the hospital after my blood counts reached normal levels and remained stabilized there for a few days, and I was also scheduled for a follow-up visit with my doctor in a month to check on the ovary and the abdominal fluid levels.

I sat there amazed at how quickly things had turned around for the better. "My blood counts came up in a few days. How in the world was that possible?" Typically it would take years to turn my blood counts around, but through faith and the excellent treatment by a doctor who is not only brilliant but is a strong believer, miracles seemed to be happening – miracles that may seem small to the world but were huge to us. My blood counts did not usually turn around so quickly like this, not ever – God is amazing! I realized then just how critical a combination of medicine and spirituality is to the human needs in this world, and I pray that God will work through Dr. Sweiss to lead the way for others in the medical profession.

I trusted that the ovarian cancer would work out somehow, and I knew to stay focused on the blessings that were in front of us at the moment. More and more it was obvious that "... *With man this is impossible, but with God ALL things are possible*" *(Matthew 19:26)*.

CHAPTER 19

Power of Prayer

(Age 38)

"Blessed is the man who perseveres under trial, because when he has stood the test, he will receive the crown of life that God has promised to those who love him" (James 1:12).

Four days after returning home from the hospital with the internal bleeding from the ovarian cyst, I found myself suddenly overcome with severe abdominal pain and a high fever. I was up all night and by morning called my doctor. She was concerned that I had internal bleeding again and wanted me to go to the closest emergency room. I wanted to cry, but I prayed instead, trusting God to heal me and thanking Him for the blessings just a few short days ago. Instead of going to the University of Chicago, Chris loaded me in the car and we headed to a local ER in hopes of being seen there sooner than I would be seen in a major trauma ER unit in the city.

Unfortunately, the week of March 19th obviously was one of complete madness and chaos. The ER rooms and hospitals were full around the city and suburbs. I found myself waiting for three hours in the waiting room. I lay on the couch in severe pain hoping to be seen soon. When I was finally called back I explained my complicated medical history and all that had transpired the week before. I was put in a bed in the hallway of the ER and pretty much left there. Thank goodness for Chris, who had taken over the nurse role as well helping me with everything I needed. I was in a lot of pain and feeling very sick. When the doctor said they wanted to do an abdominal CT scan and asked me to drink the contrast liquid, the thought turned my stomach. Once again, I could barely get one cup down. My stomach would have no part of it no matter how hard I tried. It was at least the fourth time I was facing a situation of not being able to drink the CT liquid contrast.

The doctors decided to do an ultrasound of the abdomen and ovaries as well. Again, it showed a lot of fluid, just like the week before. The doctors realized a local hospital was not the place for a complicated patient such as me so they put in a request to transfer me downtown to the University of Chicago.

We sat in the ER for twelve hours before they transferred me by ambulance to the U of C ER. It was a grueling ride, with every bump sending stabbing pains through my abdomen despite the IV morphine drip they had started in an effort to ease my pain. It brought back memories from years ago when I felt like the muscles were being ripped from my bones that time when I was loaded in an ambulance in excruciating pain to be transferred to the University of Chicago. I found out later I was the last patient accepted that day into the U of C ER. They had gone into "hold" status on account of the over abundance of accidents, illnesses, gunshot wounds, etc. that had flooded the ER and hospital rooms that week. The first blessing in this second round of my March 2007 journey, I was able to get into the hospital where I needed to be. Looking back today, I cannot imagine what would have happened to me if they had turned me away.

The doctors immediately started pulling blood work and determining what tests they wanted to do. They kept me on IV morphine for the pain. I had to go through repeat ultrasounds and abdominal CT scans. My white blood count was dangerously high as well as my liver enzymes were off the charts (bilirubin of 11.7). I was screaming yellow. It looked as if Samantha had taken a yellow marker and colored every part of me, including the whites of my eyes. It was unbelievable! All of that bile in my system made me feel even more sick, so they were giving me anti-nausea medicine along with the morphine. I lay there just wanting all of this to be over. My heart was breaking as I watched Chris trying to desperately grab a few minutes of sleep in the chair next to my bed. We had been in the ER for two days waiting for a hospital bed to become available. Once again, God gave me the strength to somehow endure these things, but to see the pain it causes those who care about me is difficult to handle.

The doctors were not saying a whole lot but things obviously turned to a very serious point because they said they were waiting for an available bed in ICU for me. I thought, *ICU?* They then brought in a team of ICU doctors to be with me in the ER until they could get me transferred. I was pretty out of it with the morphine, so I'm not really sure what exactly was going on. I knew they said I had an infection in my abdomen so they started IV antibiotics. They also started high dose steroids to help with any blood disease activity that might be happening (based on the amount of jaundice it seemed my disease was in a very hyper state again). At midnight I finally was transferred to an ICU room where the nurses and ICU team of doctors were absolutely phenomenal. They let Chris stay in the room with me but again, no bed or anything comfortable for him to sleep on – just a chair with a stool that he could try to spread out on. That was not easy for a 6' 3" man! I felt so bad for him, but I knew he did not want to leave my side, and I didn't want him to either.

I was constantly monitored with blood counts, heart monitors, and multiple medications being changed through the IV bag – there was constant activity, it seemed. I had multiple teams of doctors watching me from many departments: ICU, Hematology/Oncology, Gynecology, Surgery, and Rheumatology. Based on the ultrasounds/abdominal CT scans that showed a lot of fluid, a tumor in my ovary and the ovarian cancer marker (CA125, I think) being elevated, all signs were pointing to advanced stage ovarian cancer. Apparently the follow-up was indicating very strongly that this was ovarian cancer, so the doctors discussed that with us. I thought Chris was going to cry. It seemed after all of these years he was at his end. I prayed, *Please Jesus, don't put him through this anymore. He deserves so much better.*

The doctors decided it was important to go into the abdomen and extract some of the fluid in order to obtain the answers they required for proper treatment. I continued to receive a lot of pain medicine, high dose steroids and a combination of antibiotics through the IV, but my blood counts were not improving. My bones began to ache worse than you could ever imagine; I felt as if I had no strength left in my muscles at all. I finally insisted that Chris go home that night so that he could get some rest. He looked exhausted, both mentally and physically. I was afraid to send him home because I felt very ill. I didn't know what could happen in the middle of the night, but I wanted him to rest. If something happened to me, I wanted him to be there with the kids. My heart ached for them so much it was almost unbearable.

After my 2 am blood draw, I found myself just lying in bed crying. I was crying not only from the pain and being sick, but also my heart was breaking from being away from my kids. Even beyond that, however, I felt overwhelmed with that feeling again of *this is it ... I'm not sure I have the strength to go on this time.* The thought of all that I would leave behind, including two young children who would be left motherless, ached to my soul. I vowed to myself, *I cannot give up; I have to trust in His plan.*

Despite my strong faith, there aren't many Bible verses that I can recite off the top of my head. However, I had found lately that I would turn to the Bible more and more for answers. We all know how prayers combined with a complete belief truly can produce miracles. I had asked Chris to bring my Bible not knowing just how desperately I would need it that night. As I lay there crying, wanting so much to be spared from the horrible ache in my bones, I prayed for God to show me something in the Bible that would give me the strength I needed. Out of over 2,000 pages in my Bible I opened right to Psalm 6, which reads:

> *" ... O Lord, heal me, for my bones are in agony.*
> *My soul is in anguish. How long, O Lord how long?*
> *Turn, O Lord, and deliver me; save me because of your*
> *unfailing love. No one remembers you when he is dead.*
> *Who praises you from the grave? I am worn out from*
> *groaning; all night long I flood my bed with weeping*
> *and drench my couch with tears. My eyes grow weak*
> *with sorrow; they fail because of all my foes ... The Lord*
> *has heard my cry for mercy; the Lord accepts*
> *my prayer" (Psalm 6:2-9).*

Again, being overcome with that feeling of peace that is hard to describe, I started to drift off to sleep. I woke up to a beeping sound that seemed to be coming from over my head. I pushed my nurse button so the nurse could come in and check my IV pumps because that is what the beeping sounded like, but everything was fine. They were not beeping. She searched my room for some time and even brought in another nurse to look. They could find nothing. They called maintenance. I sat there in bed and felt as if God was saying, *Sandi, pay attention something big is going to happen!* I kind of shook my head but knew in my heart something big was happening, something very big. Awhile later, the maintenance guy showed up and looked around the room. He saw an IV pump that was sitting behind the head of my bed that was beeping, but it was NOT plugged in. The nurse looked puzzled because that was an IV pump that had a dead battery, but yet it had been going off constantly for quite awhile. I smiled and drifted off to sleep as I thought, *God, I hear you, and I am paying attention. I promise I will share the testimony of what you are doing.*

I was awakened for another blood draw at 6 am. An ultrasound was scheduled for early morning so a sample of the fluid could be obtained and a plan to fight the cancer could be put into place. Time was of the essence regarding treatment. Just as the blood draw was completed it seemed there was a knock on my door from the ultrasound technician. He wheeled in the ultrasound machine, which they would use to properly locate the fluid that would be taken out by needle aspiration. The ultrasound technician was obviously irritated because they ordered this STAT and thus had pulled him out of his normal routine to deal with this. He probed (not so gently) all over my abdomen and did so multiple times – each time with more of an aggravated look on his face. He walked out of my room and said to the doctors in a very irritated tone, "I am so glad you rushed me up here for THIS; there is no fluid in her abdomen." The doctors came into the room to confirm what he was saying because it could not be possible. They did not believe what they were seeing. All of the fluid within my abdomen and the tumor on my ovary were gone! Yes G-O-N-E as in disappeared! The doctors knew there had to be fluid around the ovary still because fluid from cancer does not disappear without being removed or treated.

They transferred me to the gynecology department to have the same technician that had done the ultrasound previously perform it again. The technician could not believe her eyes. The picture had completely changed. I smiled at her and said, "God sent me a miracle." She smiled and nodded, "It sure looks that way. I can't believe what I am seeing." The doctors shared with us that they could not explain it, but there was no longer fluid around the ovary and, as far as that goes, no tumor in the ovary either. They kept talking, checking, and re-checking the ovary with the ultrasound as if they could not believe what was right in front of them. Their training certainly didn't explain anything like this. The ultrasound image from the previous week, and also a couple days prior, had completely changed – so much in fact that they ordered another ultrasound follow-up for a few weeks later to confirm the medical findings of the tumor and fluid being gone.

The doctors explained that I had a few infections at the same time – one within my abdomen, ovary, and kidneys. They also told me that my bone marrow had shut down. As a result, my body could not produce the cells needed to fight the infection. It also could not replenish the blood cells which my blood disease was killing off. Now the ICU made complete sense, and I understood why my bones ached so much! I was fighting for my life. That day my blood counts started to return to normal. I was released from the hospital a couple of days later. I couldn't believe that within a couple of days I had gone from facing death in ICU to walking out of the hospital.

A month later, the follow-up ultrasound confirmed that the obvious signs of advanced stage ovarian cancer had completely resolved without any medical treatment. God had sent us a miracle. I was in awe.

CHAPTER 20

Blessings Too Good

(Age 39)

"I will make you into a great nation and I will bless you; I will
make your name great, and you will be a blessing. I will bless
those who bless you, and whoever curses you I will curse; and all
people on earth will be blessed through you" (Genesis 12: 2-3).

When I was facing the lymphoma diagnosis in 2005, Tyler said to me with tears in his eyes, "Mom, God could not possibly send you another miracle. He has used up too many on you already. How will you pull through this one too?" It was another opportunity for me to remind him that with God all things are possible … there are no limits when it comes to God's undying love for us once we accept Christ into our hearts.

The blessings that we receive seem too good to be true because a whole new world opens up for us. We gain a whole new perspective! We begin to see things differently than we did before. When we trust God with every aspect of our life, we do our best to live in His way. His way challenges us to be good people – the people God made each of us to be.

It is easier to be angry than it is to fill our hearts with love; it is easier to judge than to be supportive in situations we may not understand; it is easier to be hateful than empathetic or compassionate. However, if we can rise above all of that and meet the challenge of being more like Christ, we find our decisions and actions fill our hearts with peace and happiness instead of bitterness, which poisons us. Soon our lives begin to fall into place, and challenges that once seemed overwhelming are manageable because we have a renewed strength that is hard to describe.

> *"The knowledge of the secrets of the kingdom of heaven has been given to you, but not to them. Whoever has will be given more, and he will have an abundance. Whoever does not have, even what he has will be taken from him. This is why I speak to them in parables:*
>
> *'Though seeing, they do not see; though hearing, they do not hear or understand.' In them is fulfilled the prophecy of Isaiah: 'You will be ever hearing but never understanding: you will be ever seeing but never perceiving. For this people's heart has become calloused; they hardly hear with their ears, and they have closed their eyes. Otherwise they might see with their eyes, hear with their ears, understand with their hearts and turn, and I would heal them.'*
>
> *But blessed are your eyes because they see, and your ears because they hear. For I tell you the truth, many*

prophets and righteous men longed to see what you see
but did not see it, and to hear what you hear but
did not hear it" (Matthew 13:11-17).

An abundant life is waiting for each of you … all you have to do is open your mind and allow your eyes to see it and perceive it and your ears to hear it and understand it. God is patiently waiting for you to accept Christ into your heart so that He can pour all of His blessings into your life.

When we help others, whether it is a simple act of kindness, a charity donation, volunteering time, or sharing personal experiences to offer support and guidance, God is working through us. God does not physically stand before us and give food to the poor. Instead He tugs on our hearts, guiding us to take the food to the poor. Each one of us has that tug, it is up to us whether we ignore or listen to it. Are you listening? If not, start listening, and the blessings you will receive will seem too good to be true.

~~~~~~~~~~

I was oblivious to how God works through so many different avenues to reach us. Once I started opening my eyes, my ears, my mind, and my heart to Him, the things that seemed impossible were suddenly possible. I am still in awe at the blessings that have unfolded in my life; blessings which are truly too good to be true and, yes, that includes every challenge!

I have prayed for some time asking God to help me figure out my purpose in life. I think we all wonder that, don't we? I knew my heart seemed a little different than most, especially through these challenges. Many looked at me as if I was crazy when I would say I felt blessed with each challenge that God sent my way. It was because I was excited to see what He was going to do next, what testimony would be revealed proving that God does exist and what He can do in our lives when we believe and trust in Him. The neat part was that by being this way even before realizing the importance of each of these true testimonies, my experiences were helping those close to me find their way to Him, in a way that wasn't preaching or "Bible thumping," as some negatively refer to it, but instead through experiencing it with me as it unfolded along my spiritual path.

I had countless people tell me how important it was to share my true-life experiences with the world, because what better way to prove that God exists? I continued to pray about it. Prior to my surgery in November, my husband and I decided to get baptized again but in our new church, Parkview. We love our church and feel so blessed that God helped us to find it. We were both baptized as babies, but there was real power in making a decision as an adult to prove to the world our belief in Christ by accepting Him again into our hearts through baptism. I get chills just thinking about how powerful that baptism was to me, and the fact that we were baptized by Pastor Lonnie is also very special to me. He has some incredible testimonies of his own. The stories he shared during church were very inspirational to me because they were true-life experiences and, as a result, touched the hearts of many. I continued to pray that God would help me find my way to my true purpose here on earth.

Shortly before the surgery I had another incredible dream/vision. God was talking to me again just as He had years ago when He worked through Ken to get me back on my spiritual path. God was telling me, *you are special, and you do have a purpose here.* I sat there looking at Him in awe yet also feeling puzzled knowing that I believe each of us has a purpose here, but I wasn't sure what my purpose was exactly. He then reached out His hands towards me, and in His hands was this magnificent, beautiful, warm, indescribable ball of light. It was so real. I sat there in awe, not feeling worthy of His presence. He reached down, and as He was placing the light into my heart, He said to me, "You are my special child. Now it is time for you to go and do your work for me." I woke up with chills, looking around the room to see if He was still there. It was so real and powerful being in His presence – so much that I felt weak in my knees and couldn't get up for awhile. I just sat and prayed and cried. I did not feel worthy of this. I thought, *Who am I to have a light put inside of me?* It took me a couple of weeks to actually open up about this vision to anyone.

I then had my surgery, and it was during my recovery when Tyler nudged me to get my book finished. I still felt unworthy of that dream, and then while I was praying for guidance to find a Bible verse for one of my new chapters I came across this verse:

"For God, who said, 'Let light shine out of darkness,'
made his light shine in our hearts to give us the light of
the knowledge of the glory of God in the face of Christ"
(2 Corinthians 4:6).

I realized then what God was trying to tell me. All I had been through and all of the experiences, including finding Parkview Church, provided me the knowledge I needed to find and know God … to accept Him completely so that I could share that knowledge with others. I had no idea just how much I would learn facing adversity or how important a church would be to helping me understand God better. I now had the "light of the knowledge" of God through Christ filling my heart. I still have much to learn but feel He has prepared me for the next step in my journey. It is time to share His Word and my experiences with anyone who will listen!

I pray every day that God will open up the avenues and allow me to share these incredible testimonies through whatever channels will help others. I do not know the specifics of what God has planned for me, but I know He has a plan. I trust completely in His plan, and I am excited to be part of it! I pray that you have found inspiration in reading my story and that God blesses you along your journey of faith. I continue in my walk of faith, and every day I pray that somehow I can help others find their way to Him. May you accept Christ into your heart and allow Him to pour His many blessings upon you!

"I rejoice greatly in the Lord that at last you have renewed your concern for me. Indeed you have been concerned, but had no opportunity to show it. I am not saying this because I am in need, for I have learned to be content whatever the circumstances. I know what it is to be in need, and I know what it is to have plenty, I have learned the secret of being content in any and every situation, whether well fed or hungry, whether living in plenty or in want. I can do everything through him who gives me strength" (Philippians 4:10-13).

References

[1]KIDdiddles.com (1998). Song Lyrics. Retrieved December 30, 2007 from http://www.kididdles.com/lyrics/j008.html.

[2]Biblical Proportions (2004). *The Life of St. Christopher.* Retrieved December 30, 2007 from http://www.biblicalproportions.com/modules/ wfsection/article.php?articleid=4761&page=1.

[3]American Red Cross. *Give Blood – The Gift of Life.* Retrieved December 30, 2007 from http://www.redcross.org/donate/give/. 1-800-GIVE-LIFE

[4]Fishback-Powers, Margaret (1998). *Footprints: Scripture with Reflection Inspired by the Best-Loved Poem.*

[5]*Finding God.* ICBS, Inc. (1998-2008). Retrieved February 27, 2008 from http://www.1stholistic.com/prayer/A2007/spirituality-finding-god.htm

Barker, Kenneth, Donald Burdick, John Stek, Water Wessel, Ronald Youngblood (1995). *The NIV Study Bible, 10th Anniversary Edition.*

Community Bible Church (2004). *Inspirational Stories Site.* Retrieved November 30, 2007 from http://www.community-bible-church.org/inspire.html.

Grace and Mercies Website. Retrieved December 30, 2007 from http://www.graceandmercyministries.co.uk/christian_jokes.htm.

The Official Footprints in the Sand page (2003). Footprints in the Sand. Retrieved December 9, 2007 from http://www.footprints-inthe-sand.com/. Rights to copy poem obtained from author in February 2008.

Printed in the United States
204162BV00001B/133-189/P

9 781606 471098